South Carolina Ghosts

Into the moss-draped forest of Daufuskie Island.

South Carolina Ghosts
From the Coast to the Mountains

By Nancy Roberts

University of South Carolina Press

**Other University of South Carolina Press Books
by Nancy Roberts**

The Haunted South
Where Ghosts Still Roam

Ghosts of the Carolinas

Ghosts of the Southern Mountains and Appalachia

The Gold Seekers
Gold, Ghosts and Legends from Carolina to California

North Carolina Ghosts & Legends

Civil War Ghost Stories & Legends

© 1983 University of South Carolina Press

Published in Columbia, South Carolina, by the
University of South Carolina Press

First Printing 1983

Manufactured in the United States of America

15 14 13 12 11 10 9 8 7 6   16 15 14 13 12

ISBN 0-87249-428-4 (hard back)
ISBN 0-87249-429-2 (pbk.)

Library of Congress Catalog Card Number 84-106051

Contents

Preface

The stories in this collection are based upon actual events. In some cases names have been changed to protect the privacy of the living or relatives of the deceased but every effort has been made to check the veracity of those interviewed. When stories have been related in several versions, the earliest and most authentic has been selected.

To the best of the writer's knowledge and research each account has a sound factual basis. If some bear a resemblance to other stories, it is because the similarity of real-life experiences and emotions necessarily produces tales in many different areas which share important structural aspects.

As these stories transcend time and place and move from the ancient world to the present they undergo transformations, but here and there we glimpse a common thread that ties us to the thoughts of our long-ago ancestors. Time is eclipsed and for a moment there occurs, even in the most sophisticated of us, a flashback into the mind of archetypal man.

In the fourth century Salustius declared, "Myths are something which never happened but always are." The word "myth" is used here not to say that an event is untrue but simply that as yet, we do not know how to explain it.

But one thing is certain. Late at night the ghosts begin to stir!

Acknowledgment

I would like to thank my husband Jim Brown
for his enthusiasm in helping me locate some of
these stories. His constant encouragement has meant
a great deal in the completion of this book.

I

The Ghost Hand

Summerville is one of South Carolina's most inviting towns with its tree-lined streets and picturesque old Victorian homes surrounded by banks of azaleas. Ken and Ann Royal thought about one of these houses for a long time. It was a large, ornate white house on Main Street and five years ago they finally bought it. Ken, who is an accountant, felt he wanted to make Summerville a permanent home. The Royals had no idea their dream house was haunted.

There is more than one story of a house with supernatural happenings in Summerville but this haunting is still going on, this month, this week, perhaps, even tonight. Ken and Ann's original disbelief in ghosts is changing.

The house was built by the McNairs who lived here for many years. Mrs. Robert McNair died in it and whatever the cause of her demise there is no hint of foul play. Did she breathe her last in one of those high four-poster beds such as the one that now occupies the Royal's front bedroom? It is very likely she did. Shortly after her death there were rumors that she had buried a tremendous sum of money somewhere on the grounds. If so, it has never been found.

In those days there was a stable back of the house and this area was later cemented over with four inches of concrete. If a treasure is buried there it would be most difficult to reach. After the McNair's era and before the Royals bought it, the house was rented briefly.

Ann is a warm, attractive woman in her thirties with a talent for homemaking. Her taste and decorator touch is apparent in every room for there are bright, cheerful colors and carefully selected antiques. But despite its homey look and the affection the family shares for this house, there are times when they have been badly frightened here.

Ten-year-old Sharon was the first to experience anything unusual.

"One night Sharon called me into her room," says Mrs. Royal, "and said, 'Mother, there's a man in my room.' I thought she must be dreaming. I turned on her bathroom light and said 'You just had a bad dream.'

" 'No mother, I really saw him. He was standing here near my bed.' She was badly frightened. I remember opening her closet door to show her no one was in the room because she kept insisting a man was there. It wasn't until later that I thought about that night.

"It was after Ken told me of the footsteps in the hall. I was asleep and he was up late watching the Johnny Carson show. Then he heard someone walking in the hall and went out there to see who it was. A tall, dark figure was going into the dining room. Of course, he followed turning on all the lights, checking both the dining room and the kitchen but he could find no one.

"My mother lives in an apartment upstairs and the next morning I told her about it. She sat down and said, 'Oh, Ann, I've been wanting to tell you what happened to me but I was afraid you all would think I was crazy. I have seen that figure three times and he has touched me!

" 'The first time I saw it, I was asleep with one hand resting palm upward on my pillow. Suddenly, I was awakened by the sensation of something ice cold in my hand. I turned my head and looked and resting in my palm were these two huge white hands in a position of prayer and a man in a black trench coat was leaning over me. His hands were only a few inches from my face. When I opened my eyes and stared at his hands he pulled them away and as I reached for my bedside lamp he disappeared.'

"As mother told me about it I could see by her face that she must have been terrified. What an experience!

"One of the most recent appearances of the ghost hap-

At first she thought she must be having a nightmare—but she was wide awake and the man was real!

pened on a night when my husband was working late, our daughter was out babysitting and our son Don was here at home watching television. It was about ten o'clock and I thought I would go ahead and get my bath so I told him, 'If the phone rings, please get it for me.' Then I went in to take my shower. I was drying my hair when I heard the dog just raising cain. She was barking like crazy and I thought it was Kenneth coming in because sometimes she gets all excited when she hears him.

"I didn't think any more about it but when I came out of the bathroom into the bedroom the dog was looking under the bed and barking as hard as she could. It gave me a very strange feeling and I went into the den to see if Ken had come home. Don was lying on the floor in front of the television asleep and when I called my husband there was no answer. He was not in the house.

"The dog kept right on barking at something under the bed and by then I was thoroughly frightened. I thought, someone is under that bed and I'm not about to go see who it is! I called Ken at the office and he had already left. One of the men that answered said, 'You talk to me and don't get off that phone because if there is someone in the house they probably won't bother you as long as you are talking to me on the phone. Ken should be home any minute.'

"I stayed on the phone and then I heard our German shepherd barking louder than ever. From where I sat I could see the hall. The dog was out there now barking and growling and soon I heard the den door open and shut. Whoever or whatever it was had left and the dog stopped barking. I heard Ken's car and when he came in we searched the house. Nothing was missing. Both of my diamond rings were on the top of the chest of drawers and if he had wanted to take them he could have.

"That same week I was in the kitchen and my pantry door opened and then shut for no apparent reason. I was the only person in the house. As I stood in front of the sink I caught the movement of the pantry door out of the corner of my eye. It was slowly opening. I turned and just as I turned the door closed. One of the children must be playing a trick on me, I thought and immediately went over and opened it to see who was in there. There was no one.

"But the most frightened I have ever been was one night a few weeks ago. I had gotten up about two o'clock and walked down the hall to get something for my sinuses. I took a teaspoon and went back to bed. Right after I had gotten into bed and closed my eyes, I began to have this funny feeling that someone was watching me. Have you ever felt that way?

"I opened my eyes and there he was—this dark figure. You don't see any facial features. It was at night and there was just enough light from the lamp outside for me to see this tremendous figure of a man, a man in a long black coat. He reached out a huge, white, stubby-fingered hand and I thought he was coming for my throat. It scared me to death! I screamed and screamed and as I did he vanished just as if he had gone down beneath the bed.

"I'll never forget that hand as long as I live. He was standing right by my bed. We've got this old Charleston four poster rice bed.

"The dog began barking and, of course, the whole house got up. We were sure it was a prowler. We checked the entire house, doors, windows, everything and nothing had been disturbed so we knew it had to be something here inside this house with us. But what could we do?

"About three weeks ago mother saw him for the third time. One afternoon he appeared in broad daylight. She was sitting in her living room and caught a glimpse of a figure walking through her bedroom. By the time she had gotten in there no one was there and she told herself it must have been a shadow. But a few minutes after she sat back down, she saw something go back by the doorway. This time it was more like a black cloud but you could tell it was a person.

"It was not until after we had seen the ghost that the people who had rented the house before we bought it called one night and said they had heard we had seen the ghost. I said to her, 'Well, before I tell you what I saw, would you please describe the ghost to me.'

"Her description was of a man in a long, black coat, a man with huge hands but she could never see the details of his face. Where his face should be was just a blur. It was exactly as I had seen and I had told no one the particulars. She was sleeping in the room right behind my bedroom and waked up to see the ghost standing in her doorway. Then it turned and went back out in the hall. She jumped out of bed and followed it. It was a man in a black coat. He walked up the hall and into her parent's bedroom, that's Ken and mine now, and when she came into the room it disappeared."

Ken and Ann wonder what the reason could be for the ghost's appearance. Was the house built on the site of an earlier building where some violent deed took place? Did one of the many pirates who once roamed the South Carolina coast take his ill-gotten gains with him and settle here? And does the ghost of one of his murderous comrades continue to return for his share of the treasure?

All the Royals are able to do is to put up with the presence of their dark visitor and remind themselves, as Ann Royal says, that "He has not as yet harmed any of us."

II

The Mysterious Land's End Light

The visitor to the South Carolina lowcountry comes away with memories of proud plantation homes, avenues of oaks, magnificent columned residences on East Bay or the battery, rows of rainbow-hued town houses, elegant food and colorfully turbaned black women selling the beautiful baskets produced for generations along the coast.

They are seldom aware of the bedrock of superstition and the stories of the supernatural imbedded deep in the life patterns of many South Carolinians. This is a state where people feel strongly about everything, their politics, their history and their ghosts. There is the unspoken influence of the conjure or root doctor, the plat-eye or ghost dog, and the shutters and doors painted blue to keep out ghosts and spirits.

In almost every town there is some ghostly phenomenon that defies explanation and this is the case at St. Helena's Island near Beaufort.

In early April of 1982 I began intensive research on this book and, as often occurs, while researching one story I was told about another. Dee Fitzsimmons, a young policewoman at Hilton Head Island, had formerly been stationed at Beaufort. One night when she was off duty she drove over to St. Helena's Island to look for the famous light, but saw nothing. Her next trip was another story. She had been visiting a friend on St. Helena's and as she was driving down Land's End Road she was amazed to see a light appear with a startling, fiery flash, go right through the car ahead of her and dart off to the right where it was lost in the woods beside the road!

Dee knew that she had seen the mysterious light but she had not anticipated being so scared. No matter how she tried to find a rational explanation she could not; and for a practical young woman who asked questions, received sensible answers, and dealt in the concrete world of law enforcement, an experience she could not explain was unnerving.

That night she returned to her trailer home and sat down to read and relax. Since she was unable to sleep she read longer than she intended. If it had not been for her wakefulness she probably would not have heard the light sound of footsteps outside her trailer. She went to the kitchen which was in darkness and pulled the curtain aside very slightly. A few feet away stood a strange man.

Ordinarily, the young policewoman would have been more aggressive and handled the situation herself but the experience of the light coupled with that of a would-be intruder was more than her nerves were up to that night. She called the police to come check. Dee laughs about that now but she does not laugh about seeing the Beaufort light. "It was real and I'll never forget it!"

If I had any doubts about including the story of the light in the book, they were gone after a conversation with the Hilton Head Fire Chief. We first talked of the Blue Lady of Hilton Head. He had heard of her but never seen her. But he had seen the Beaufort light.

By now my interest was thoroughly aroused and I decided to drive over to Beaufort. By the time we arrived I was tired. It was the end of a long day with two fascinating Hilton Head ghost stories for my efforts. A good book and my motel room bed held more appeal at the moment than a "ghost" light somewhere out on a country road. Even ghost hunting has its doldrums and my enthusiasm of the afternoon had fled.

If it had not been for a certain tenacity of purpose that sometimes drives me beyond the bounds of both common sense and fatigue, I would have said two ghosts were enough for one day and headed for our motel.

The ruins of the Chapel of Ease. After setting the camera up on a tripod and taking a time exposure, it was exciting to find a light to the right of the chapel. Ghost lights do register on film!

Instead, it was on to St. Helena. Crossing the bridge at Beaufort we drove on until we reached a tiny community called Frogmore. Our instructions from the policewoman and the fireman had been to turn right at a sign which would say "Land's End Road." In the morning the name of the road would have been commonplace. At night it had a disquieting ring of finality.

But what was there to fear? A ghost light some said was caused by a Confederate soldier who, decapitated by Union forces, continued to hunt for his head? I have heard likelier stories than this. Surely, he was a real bumbler if he had not found it after a century and permanently retired to the world beyond.

On the other hand there was a story of a bus full of migrant workers coming home after dusk, a fight on the bus and a distracted driver who ran the bus squarely into one of the gigantic live oak trees beside the road killing himself and several passengers. Which story was true, or was either? I wondered. There was a place I had been told was a good place to park but I couldn't seem to find it. A country store came up on my left but I didn't stop.

The fireman had mentioned an old church called the Chapel of Ease. Perhaps, it was there we were to park and wait for the light to appear. Good, it must be the white building gleaming in the moonlight. I pulled the car over to the left and into what I believed was a church yard. But there was a shock awaiting me.

Now, the moon had passed from beneath its cloud cover and shone upon the most eerie ruins I had ever seen and there we were in the midst of them! On one side the ragged white shell of the old chapel, its windows mere empty, dark holes. On the right was an ancient cemetery unused for years, and set off apart from the place of the living and the dead was a dark mausoleum with a black hole gouged in its front by those who would rob a family tomb! What a place to stay and await the arrival of a ghost light.

Our stay must have been no more than a quarter of an hour but it seemed an eternity. We continued down the road all the way to Land's End. A turn to the right and we were headed toward the old fort. Was night really the time to visit it? A reporter at the Beaufort paper had mentioned that sometimes the light had been seen wandering about the fort. There was the great dark entrance. Above it the sheer concrete walls were full of shadowy shapes outlined by artful strokes of moonlight.

Did the light appear along the crest of the fort with the woods and sea beyond? Did it rise from the water and drift upward through the trees? I was midway up the rungs of an iron ladder imbedded in the wall of the old fort when a cloud passed over the moon leaving all in utter blackness, the thick, humid darkness so dense it became a heavy, smother-

*An old mausoleum is the only other building left at the
ruins of the Chapel of Ease.*

ing cloak. I had reached the top of the ladder but could not see enough to risk exploring further. Below was the steep drop to the floor of the fort, before me was the forest. Suddenly, I heard an incredibly weird sound. A high pitched shriek rose to a startling crescendo and then faded in the air. Every tiny hair on my body rose and I was chilled to the bone despite the summer night's heat.

Was there really the ghost of a man who had lost his head somewhere out here, perhaps, nearby? The moon came out again and if there was a ghost here at this fort or in the woods at least we would not meet in that impenetrable blackness. There was the path through the woods and below lay the water with a trail of moonlight across it. There was no sign of the light.

Exhausted we decided to leave and come back for more research the following day. I was filled with disappointment. As we reached the main road I suggested we drive back down the road from which we had just come one more time and stop at the little store. Ahead of us was another car driving about forty-five miles an hour. We hung back a bit to remain well behind it. There are too many curves on this road to speed or pass safely at night and the oak trees are so close to the edge of the pavement that if I had stretched my arm out the window, I could have touched their rough bark with my finger tips.

Suddenly, I saw an immense ball of fire rise in the air in front of the car ahead of us. For a moment it simply did not register and I continued talking. The second time it happened I stopped in mid-sentence and all I could say was "Look! For heavens sake, look!" It bounced up in the air a third time and the fourth time left me scarcely able to speak for the light rose again, but this time it traveled over the roof of the car ahead, toward us and then went off at a tangent into the woods at the right of the road.

Both of us saw it. There is no doubt of that. We pulled over to the side of the road and waited thinking there must be some reasonable explanation. Perhaps, there was a car coming from the opposite direction and somehow we were seeing its headlights. Ten minutes passed and no car appeared. Could it be headlights coming over a series of hills in the distance? No. This island is as flat as most of the coastal Carolina area. And nothing could explain the fact that it resembled a ball of fire that was no more than fifty to seventy-five feet away from us.

The following day we came back and interviewed people along the road. Mary Simpson who lives just beyond the Chapel of Ease has seen it many times. She believes the light began after a bus accident which she places sometime around 1948.

Lillian Chaplin who lives farther down the road on the way to Fort Fremont, which is at the tip of the island, says her father told her the light has been there since Civil War days. Mrs. Chaplin says, "The best place to see it is between Adam St. Baptist Church and the Hanging Tree. That's a double tree that hangs over the road and they say some runaway slaves were caught and hung from it."

On the way back to Frogmore we stopped at the country store and talked to Bill Brown who has lived along the road for years. He says, "Lawd, I knew that man that drove that bus. He ought to have known better than to go fast around one of those curves. Hit a tree plumb head on and killed himself and two other people. Lots of folks were hurt, too. Sometimes they say, 'That light is old Willie's bus comin' right out of the bad place.'"

A former deputy with the Beaufort County Sheriff's Department was sure he saw the phenomenon and described the light as a large white ball of fire with a reddish halo rimming the central light. The light drifted along the road with a swinging motion. Robert Cooler, the owner of a boating business and Dean Poucher, at that time with the Beaufort Chamber of Commerce, saw the Land's End Light as a large, bright light which came down the road toward them and then disappeared when they tried to approach it.

Islanders say that several years ago two Marines from Parris Island made up their minds they were going to drive right through the light and they did. But they hit a tree head on and one of them was killed. Meanwhile sightseers continue to gather to wait for the light, parking beside the road and sometimes even standing in the middle.

I don't mind admitting that on the night I drove down Land's End Road, I saw something I have never seen on any other road in any part of the United States. Whatever it is, the light is definitely there and it is a startling sight!

But, somehow, none of the stories really explain it. They just underline the fact that we continue to co-exist with the unknown.

III

The Haunted Castle at Beaufort

On the warm July day I arrived in Beaufort my mission was an unusual one for I was in search of a ghost. There should be many there for the streets of this historic town are lined with fascinating, antebellum homes. But when I turned on Craven Street and saw the tall towers and gloomy columned facade of the house on the waterfront, I felt strangely certain that this was where I would find my story.

A few hours later I was back after discovering that the house called the Castle is, indeed, linked with a ghost. This European style home built by Dr. Joseph F. Johnson in the 1850s enjoyed the reputation of being one of the finest of the lowcountry.

The house looms high above the great bend of the Beaufort River and seems to brood darkly over the past. A two-acre garden around it is filled with huge azaleas, ancient, gnarled oaks and long, tangled vines. When the tide rises a small marshy stream extends its watery arm to encircle it and create a moat. Viewed through an evening mist or the dim light under moss-draped trees, the home takes on an eerie, dreamworld quality.

As long as she could recall, Eliza, daughter of Dr. Johnson, had known the Castle was not like other houses. She had heard unaccountable noises and the mysterious opening and closing of doors when not a breath of air stirred in the humid, semitropical Beaufort night. She knew that the house had been used as a hospital by Federal troops after Fort Beauregard fell in 1861. The little laundry building had served as a morgue and just to think about it was enough to make Eliza

Mist rises about "The Castle." Beneath the front porch are the brick arches and shadowy walkways. Does the ghost still perform his antics?

shudder. She soon discovered that of all the places in this enormous three-story house, the basement was the strangest for she never seemed to feel alone there.

At first this made her uncomfortable, and as she played with her dolls she would place her back against the wall and turn their china faces toward her so she could always look out into the shadows. Sometimes she would play here with the cook's little girl who was about her age, but before they had been down there long Augusta, the girl's mother, would come.

She would bustle down the steps in all her starched dignity, and the girls would flee before her. She warned them ominously that something would surely get them in that basement. One time she said it would be a "hant" and young Eliza stared at her curiously. Was that why she had those extraordinary feelings when she was alone down there? What did a "hant" look like? Had Augusta ever seen one? She asked but Augusta just frowned, flicked her feather duster vigorously over the glass doors of the china cupboard and pretended to be too busy to answer. That was a sign to Eliza that the question had made her uncomfortable.

Eliza sought opportuniites to go down there to play but her first real chance came one hot summer day when Augusta was sick and sent word that her sister would come instead. The sister spent the morning polishing silver and cooking dinner leaving Eliza free to do as she pleased.

She would always remember that day for it was the first time her doll, Emma Belle, had ever worn the beautiful new taffeta dress her mother had given her. Emma Belle had skin white as porcelain, rosy cheeks and black hair that was never out of place for it was painted on her head. The blue dress with its tight bodice and high neck fitted to perfection. Eleven-year-old Eliza decided that she and Emma Belle would have a tea party in the basement.

Taking the doll table, a set of miniature china dishes decorated with tiny pink flowers, and leaving the door at the top of the stairs cracked ever so slightly, she and Emma Belle descended into the dimness of the cool ground floor. The house was built completely of brick which insulated it so well against the heat that the basement felt as pleasant as a spring house. Eliza sat the doll across from her and began arranging the dishes carefully on the tiny table.

Startled by what she thought must be the metallic sound of the door latch at the head of the steps, she dropped one of her little cups to the floor. She listened intently for she knew she would hear the sound of footsteps on the wide, bare floor boards if Augusta's sister had closed the door. All was quiet. When she picked up the cup she noticed its tiny handle had broken off and in her consternation thought no more about the sound.

Soon she became absorbed in making tea party chatter as she mimicked the subjects her mother and her friends discussed. Emma Belle was a good listener to her monologue on fashions, whose sons were most eligible, and the latest news from Charleston. Mrs. Johnson was an accomplished hostess and although Eliza was still young, anyone overhearing her might guess she would carry on the family tradition. She was in the midst of telling Emma about the young Charlestonian at the ball who "begged me for every dance" when suddenly she stopped and stared over the doll's head.

Her blue eyes widened until they were almost round but she did not move or cry out. Quite near her stood a tiny, wizened little old man. He wore a cap closely fitted about his face, brightly colored shirt, tight britches and pointed shoes. His antics were so ridiculous that she was tempted to laugh rather than be afraid. There was the faint, silvery tinkle of bells and then, in the flick of an eyelid, he was gone. It was not long afterward that Eliza passed the age when doll parties were absorbing and the visits to the basement ceased. She did not see the little man as much as feel his presence or sometimes hear the sound of his bells ever so faintly.

As she grew up her friends affectionately called her "Lilly," and the more prosaic name of Eliza was used less and less. She and her husband gave many gay parties and one of the party pastimes was often a table rapping session. It was a popular fad and if not evidence of the supernatural, at least was amusing. Between the double stairways of the house, Lilly and her guests would gather around a table, place their hands upon it and ask questions.

The table would rap back spelling out answers by the number of raps. But one night the words could not be understood. They were obviously in a foreign language no one present could translate. A guest knew a linguistics expert at a large university and suggested the words be sent to him. Lilly Danner was inquisitive enough to do so and the answer came back, "These words are archaic French." By now, Lilly knew who the little man was and she was sure it was his spirit that had spoken.

As the story is told, when settlers led by Frenchman, Jean Ribaut, came ashore in 1562 a jester who was a dwarf accompanied them. The little fellow was later hanged, it may be by the cruel Captain Albert de la Pierria, and the dwarf's spirit wandered over the marsh and sand sea isles for some 280 years. When the European style mansion was constructed by Dr. Johnson, Guenache, as the jester was called, had at last found a place that reminded him of home. He moved into the ground floor soon after it was completed and is said to have been seen over the years.

None of this disturbed Mrs. Danner who is remembered in Beaufort to this day as very much the grande dame. She was a spirited lady who would shoot from the upstairs porch at anyone who came into her yard after dark, gave up her mourning earlier than the other ladies of her day, and dyed her hair a bright red right up until the time of her death in her nineties.

Lilly Danner's successors in the Castle were her nephew Howard E. Danner and his wife Ruby. Ruby Danner recalls her experience with the spirit which occurred one rainy night when clouds of white mist from the river lay thick about the house and over the garden. In an upstairs bedroom adjacent to the portico her grandson was sick in bed. Mrs. Danner was in her room across the hall when she heard the screen door slam in the boy's room.

She darted into his room calling out, "You ought to be in bed, Danner. Come in from the porch this instant," but there lay the boy snug in his bed and only seconds after the door slammed.

"I haven't been up, grandmother. Who was that old man who went out the screen door?" She knew it must have been Guenache.

Over the years there have been stories of encounters with the little dwarf, and even today the Castle retains its air of dark mystery. The great sentinel oak, now twenty feet in girth, stands guard before the steps. Beneath the front porch are the brick arches, the shadowy walkway and behind it the basement. Does Guenache still perform his antics on certain rare occasions in the Castle? Is the silvery sound of his bells sometimes heard when the mist curls like smoke about the lower floor of the house? Who will see him next and will they dare to say, I saw the dwarf, Guenache, today?

IV

The Hitchhiker of Route 107

Sometimes, after interviewing a number of people, it is necesary to select the most likely central figure in an extraordinary drama. No one is quite certain of Larry Stevens' age, although most guess that he was about thirty. During the 1950s Stevens kept a small plane at the Greenville-Spartanburg airport.

A solitary sort of chap, he always flew alone and often wore a shabby, black raincoat. We ask the reader's patience if the following account of Larry Stevens flight one April afternoon must include a certain amount of conjecture.

For this quiet, shy young man, the bright yellow plane trimmed with black was the great adventure. When he flew he felt bolder and more daring than he ever did on the ground. That spring afternoon, his strong, thin fingers checked the plane as usual. He poked his head with the straight blond hair and his face with its long, thinish nose everywhere. And, the blazing blue eyes which were his best feature made a careful, preflight check of his aircraft. He did this even if he had just taxied up to the gas pump in perfect condition.

Stevens takeoff was smooth and in a few minutes he had left the Greenville-Spartanburg airport behind and was heading toward the mountains. As he looked down at the lush green valleys and purple shadows on the flanks of the mountains, he lost all track of time.

Finally, he found himself in the midst of that ruddy, golden light that, although it lasts only for a few minutes, transforms everything into another world that is greener, brighter, purer. Larry braked the plane as if by doing so he could savour that magical late afternoon light, hold fast to the moment, and spin it out into an eternity. Moments later the sky began to turn a smoky gray over the mountain ranges and the light had fled.

Now, the wind was rising. Not enough to worry him, just a reason for caution. Stevens knew he should be turning and heading toward Greenville. Clouds above and mountains below, it was the story of dangerous flying and like all good pilots, Larry had a healthy respect for bad weather. A few drops of rain spattered across the windshield in front of him. Then it was a downpour increasing in tempo until it drummed the top of the plane with a slow, steady roar.

All at once the sound changed and it was that of a thousand machine guns trained on his little plane. He was in the midst of a hail storm. Bouncing through the turbulent air the plane began to buck wildly. Sweat ran in rivulets down Larry's forehead, trickled across his cheeks, slid down his collar. The back of his shirt was so wet he could feel it clinging to his shoulders as he leaned forward trying to see. The weather had closed in and all he could do was fly on.

Stevens checked his compass and his heart began to pound for he was headed not in the direction of Greenville but west over the mountains. He tried to take a deep breath to calm himself. Suddenly, there was an awesome silence. The vibrating sound of the plane and even the slight quiver of the stick in his hand ceased. The engine had quit without coughing or even clearing its throat. Larry Stevens was going down and the last sound he would ever hear was that of rain pelting his plane as he watched the altimeter unwind madly.

The following morning a plane flying over the area near Walhalla saw something shiny and yellow on the side of the mountain. It was not far from Moody Springs, a natural mineral springs the U.S. Forest Service had beautified for travelers. The pilot turned back and circling near Highway 107 discovered that a small plane had gone down on the mountain. Rescuers found the aircraft damaged to such a degree it seemed impossible anyone could have survived. Search par-

The night is always dark and rainy when people pick up the hitchhiker on Route 107.

ties combed the woods. The trees were not yet in leaf making their task easier. Certainly, there must have been a pilot, yet no body was ever found.

Not long after the crash people began to tell a weird tale about a two-mile stretch of road along Highway 107. This road connects near Oconee State Park with Highway 28, the main road that leads through the South Carolina Piedmont towns of Anderson, Pendleton, Clemson, Seneca, Walhalla and on into the North Carolina mountains to Highlands.

Moody Springs is a few miles above Walhalla and two miles beyond, as you climb into the mountains, is the popular scenic Piedmont Overlook. Travelers often park here to admire the view extending for miles in the direction of Seneca and Clemson.

One rainy afternoon, interior decorator, Mike McNeil, was coming home along this road after a consultation in Highlands. He concentrated on the winding mountain road for it had begun to rain. As it grew darker the rain increased and he was relieved to note the approach to the Piedmont Overlook not far from his home. As he rounded the curve the beam of his headlights outlined the dark silhouette of a man there at the overlook. Something about the way he stood, shoulders hunched and coat collar turned up, made him appear wretched indeed. McNeil slowed and pulled over beside him.

"Need some help? I'm on my way to Walhalla and can give you a lift."

"Yes. I would certainly appreciate it," replied the man. McNeil quickly unlocked the door on the other side and pushed it open for the man to get in. He wore no hat and rivulets of water from his hair poured down across his strikingly pale face. The man sat down beside him and McNeil noticed that his black raincoat was drenched, water flowing along each fold as though they were small, winding streams. When he happened to glance at his companion's shoes he saw only a sodden, muddy mass. He could hardly tell human feet were inside them.

"I must get out at Moody Springs," his passenger said with his face turned toward the window. Moody Springs was just two miles from where he had picked him up.

"Are you sure that is where you want to get out? There's really nothing there," said McNeil, surprised.

"Oh, yes. That is where I must go if I am to be on my way home," replied the stranger. Mike tried to catch a better glimpse of his passenger's face and what he saw was so blank and expressionless that it made his skin crawl. He might as well have been riding with a dead man.

At Moody Springs his passenger got out without thanking him or even saying good-bye and it seemed as if he was borne away like a vapor upon the night air. Mike McNeil felt considerably shaken as he drove home. The next morning his car seat was still wet and a puddle of water covered the floor in front of the passenger seat.

There was one man he felt free to talk with about his experience. He drove up Highway 107 and went to the headquarters of Oconee State Park, a long, sagebrush gray building where his friend, Bob Cothran, had his office. Superintendent Cothran, a youthful appearing, brown-haired man in his fifties, leaned back in his chair and listened to McNeil's story, substantially the same one he had heard from dozens of people. Sometimes it came from campers in the park. On another occasion it was related to him by a Baptist minister who lives in the area.

One miserable, rainy night the minister saw the man standing at Moody Springs and felt sorry for him. He offered the fellow a ride and after they had started off, the man told him he wanted to go to the scenic overlook.

"But, I thought you said you were going to Greenville."

"Don't worry. I will get there," replied the stranger and he insisted on getting out of the car at the overlook despite the minister's offer of further assistance.

"It's always the same story," said Park Superintendent Cothran to McNeil. "The hitchhiker is dressed in an old raincoat and the night is a dark and rainy one which usually prompts people to pick him up. If he is picked up at the overlook he asks to be let out at Moody Springs and if he is picked up at Moody Springs, he asks to be let out at the scenic overlook. In every case, he immediately disappears as he steps away from the car. Many have seen him and he never leaves this mountain."

The only explanation the superintendent could offer is the one he heard when he arrived at the park sixteen years ago.

"In the late fifties an airplane crashed somewhere between the overlook and the springs. Its only occupant, the pilot, was never found. I understand the body of the plane was almost completely demolished by the impact. It was after that that encounters with the hitchhiker were first reported."

V

Alice of the Hermitage

There was an almost sad expression upon the face of the girl we had seen beside the road and stopped to ask directions.

"We are looking for All Saints Cemetery," I asked.

"It is just down the road a short distance," the girl answered.

"We are looking for a grave I expect all the young people know about," I said hoping she might volunteer to go with us and point it out.

She stared back at me fixedly and I noticed a delicate sort of prettiness about her face with its small features and the halo of soft hair pulled back from her forehead.

"But it will soon be dark out there in the graveyard," she replied. There was the heavy fragrance of gardenias in the air and I remember noticing for I dearly love them.

"We have a flashlight and I'm sure we can find it if you know where Alice's grave is."

"I'm sorry, but I really must be on my way," I thought I heard her say as she turned to go. We went on.

The cemetery was on our left less than a half mile down the road and we parked beside the wall. The wrought iron gate was unlocked and we pushed it open and began to shine our flashlight on first one stone and then another until we realized that unless someone were there to show us the right marker we might look far into the night and never find it.

My husband and I began to feel foolish. Here were two sane, middle-aged mid-westerners poking around out here in a South Carolina cemetery at night. We really had no idea where the grave we were looking for could be found. And, how could we be sure there had ever been a girl named "Alice?" We decided to go back to the inn.

Each year we had been coming to Litchfield Plantation in October enjoying the mild, golden autumn days and hearing a romantic story about a young girl who had died over a century ago. This trip we had become genuinely interested and the following afternoon we drove to Murrells Inlet especially to visit her home, the Hermitage, now the residence of Clarke Willcox and his wife.

Beautiful, moss-draped cedars fringed the drive that led to the Hermitage and the house itself stood looking out over an expanse of green lawn dotted with huge live oaks. Although there are many antebellum homes more impressive than this one which was built in 1849 and never meant to be ostentatious, few have survived the ravages of time any better.

Across the front porch were immense white columns over four feet around, each hewn from a massive tree. Beneath our feet the bricks of the steps felt rough and worn. They had been used as ballast to prevent sailing vessels from capsizing at sea and I couldn't help thinking that these were the same steps Alice's slippered feet had light-heartedly trod so many years before.

The Hermitage was built by Dr. Allard Belin Flagg. He chose a point of land surrounded on three sides by tidal marshes. Its front door has glass sidelights and an overhead glass transom and halfway to the back door is a second and similar door. The floors are made of twenty-foot long, heart pine boards.

Downstairs are six high ceilinged rooms, the parlor on each side of the hall decorated with dowel trim carved by apprenticed slaves. Between the two bedrooms upstairs is an unusual round window formed of curved spokes swirling out from a central eye. On the left of this window as we came upstairs was Alice's bedroom. It probably looks much as it did when she was alive, except that the personal possessions of a young girl are gone.

There are a needlework sampler over the door with the

They say that Alice still returns to her earthly home to search for her ring.

name "Alice," a spool bed with a white spread, and dainty curtains at the windows. It has a quality of simplicity and innocence which might be expected of the room of a sixteen-year-old girl. Mr. and Mrs. Willcox shared Alice's story.

Alice's last spring must have been a happy one. She was

engaged to a young man whom she loved and it was the year of her debut at Charleston's elaborate spring ball. Those who saw her commented upon her delicate beauty enhanced no doubt by dancing one waltz after another in the arms of her fiancé. But her happiness had one flaw. She was not able to admit to her parents and, particularly, her blond, headstrong brother that she was engaged. Young Allard Flagg, a physician, was very proud of his family. Like many other planters, he would have preferred that his sister marry into the planter society. Unfortunately, she had fallen in love with a young man in the turpentine industry, a mere merchant!

Aware of her brother's disapproval, Alice wore the ring on a ribbon about her neck concealing it beneath her blouse in the presence of her family. A few days after the spring ball a message arrived at the Hermitage from Alice's school. She was seriously ill. Her mother was in the mountains for it was the beginning of the dread malaria season in the lowcountry. Only her brother was at home managing the farm and visiting patients.

When he received word of Alice's illness he hurriedly equipped a carriage with everything to make her comfortable and set out for Charleston. There were rivers for the horses to ford and it was a journey of several days. By the time he was able to get her back to the Hermitage Alice was delirious. She lay tossing upon her bed too sick to make an effort to conceal the ring.

When her brother saw it, he was furious. He angrily snatched it from her neck, took it out of the house and threw it in a stream. The girl's thin, white fingers that had often grasped the ring for comfort during her illness could find it no more. And although Alice did not seem aware when her brother had removed it, she knew the ring was gone. She begged everyone who came to see her to find it and during the intervals when she was herself, it was all she talked about. So weak she could scarcely walk unsupported, she wandered about the bedroom looking for her most cherished possession.

Her brother saw her deep distress and although he was unable to accept the idea of the young man she had chosen, he was greatly disturbed lest her exertions worsen the illness. One day he made a special trip into Georgetown to find a ring that resembled the one now lying somewhere at the bottom of the stream.

"Here is your ring," he told her placing his arm about her shoulder lifting her in bed and clasping her fingers around it, but when Alice saw it she burst into tears and let the ring fall to the floor.

A few days later, her small frame wasted by illness, Alice breathed her last. She was temporarily buried in the yard of the Hermitage until her mother could arrive from the mountains. Later her body was buried in the cemetery at All Saints Waccamaw Church.

"Do you really think Alice ever comes back." I asked Mr. Willcox.

"I really don't know. Many report having seen her," said he and "I have felt her presence a number of times."

"Where is Alice's grave located in the cemetery?"

"Beyond the church on the right is a simple marble slab and upon it is engraved the name "Alice."

We sat out on the porch of the Hermitage and looked out over the salt marshes while Clarke Willcox spoke of how Alice's death had given the house a sad sort of distinction.

"People have been seeing the ghost of Alice Flagg for a hundred years. They were seeing it when I was a boy."

"And what does she do when she appears?"

"Old people in the area will tell you that she searches for her ring. I suppose she won't rest until she finds it."

"Do you think she ever returns to her bedroom here in the house?"

"My wife and I often feel her presence there," said Willcox.

"When I was growing up, just a boy really, there was an aunt of mine who slept in the room. She was looking in the mirror and brushing her hair. As she did so, she suddenly realized a young girl in a lovely white dress was reflected in the mirror beside her but when she turned, no one was there. I heard her screams as she came running down the stairs!"

He went on to say that the young people claim to have conjured up Alice's ghost out there in the old cemetery.

"They walk around her grave thirteen times backward at midnight and they say a young girl who runs around the grave nine times with her eyes closed will find that her own ring is gone."

By now, it was late afternoon and we left so that we might get to the cemetery. I did not realize how long we had spent at the Hermitage for the time had passed quickly as we listened to Clarke Willcox. The sun was already low in the sky as we drove away. We thought of waiting until next day but our visit to the Hermitage had increased our eagerness.

The light before dusk should last long enough for us to find the grave and I was convinced that, somehow, I would be drawn to the right location. I have heard people tell of a sort of sixth sense about where someone is buried, and in a perfectly strange cemetery they have been able to walk without hesitation to the grave they were seeking.

I was impatient to get there but as luck would have it, we noticed we were almost out of gas. We stopped, filled the tank and went on. It would soon be dark and I was consumed with impatience. If only the girl had been willing to help us the night before we would have found it.

Finally, we were there. I saw a chain on the gate and for a moment thought it was locked. It opened and I tried not to think, only to feel. Willcox had said Alice's grave was designated by a flat marker. Soon we would not be able to see. There was a sudden rustling sound and Ed and I both turned but it was only a stray cat leaping from a pile of leaves to perch on top of a tombstone.

We continued our search. I felt something press against my leg as I stepped over a grave and I almost screamed. How silly! It was only the cat again. Then, among the trees I saw the figure of a girl and I was sure it was the one we had met upon the road the evening before. She must have wanted to find the marker for herself. There she stood in that same long flowing dress beneath one of the live oaks. Her hair hung down in long tendrils like the Spanish moss from the tree above her. Perhaps she had found the grave already.

She turned her face and seemed to be looking at us and I waved and called. For a moment she stared back but not for long. Before we could reach her she had disappeared. My toe caught upon the edge of a stone and I would have fallen had not Ed grasped my arm. We both looked down at a white marble slab. I knelt down and with trembling fingers began to trace the words I could dimly see, A L I C E. We had found her grave.

But most exciting of all, I was sure that the girl I had just seen and the girl I had spoken to beside the road the night before were one and the same. We had seen the spirit of a lovely girl once known as Alice Bellin Flagg.

I wonder if I shall ever meet her again.

VI

The Crazy Quilt

Clouds mounted along the horizon while the sky turned an ominous, threatening yellow. All afternoon the young couple had waited for the quilt to be auctioned off. It had no planned design and most women called it a crazy quilt. Annette Larson had chosen it as a Christmas gift from her fiancé. Marble top tables, massive oak beds, china, the once loved, familiar objects of a Midwest farm family went one by one to strangers.

It seemed to Annette that the auctioneer would never pick up the quilt. She and John knew this was tornado weather and they ought to be heading home. A tornado in Great Plains country meant devastation for everything in its path and sometimes death also.

A patter of rain fell. Still they stayed on. John Gerber was a tall, shy young man with a kind way about him and he really wanted Annette to have her heart's desire. Finally, the auctioneer held up the beautiful coverlet. He started it off at ten dollars. John bid fifteen. "Twenty," came a voice from the crowd. "Twenty-five," called out John. "Thirty," signaled another bidder.

"Will anyone give me thirty-five for this fine quilt sure to bring happiness to the marriage bed?" The auctioneer smiled and waited. John raised a finger and the quilt was his.

"It is very beautiful," said the young Amishman admiringly before he handed it to Annette. The quilt was a multitude of brilliant colors. Now, it would be hers forever. Gusts of wind began to whip her skirt about her legs and even before they reached the buggy, rain poured. Annette's hair clung in long, wet tendrils about her face. Gerber whipped the horses and off they galloped at a mad pace through the deluge. The girl grew ever more pale as the wind rocked the buggy relentlessly.

The sound of the wind increased until it became a roar and suddenly there was a horrendous jolt. John Gerber felt his wagon lift off the ground and sail through the air. Seconds stretched into an eternity. Then he lost consciousness. When he recovered he was lying on the ground and all was deathly still. Amazed that he seemed unhurt, he picked himself up and looked for Annette.

At first all he saw were bits and pieces of the wagon and a tiny shred of her shawl. Why had they not left earlier? Then, perhaps, a hundred feet away he saw the brightly colored quilt. He walked over to where it lay upon the ground stretched out almost as neatly as if it had been placed upon a bed. Dazed as he was, he could not help but notice its beauty. Then, he realized something was beneath it.

With a sense of terrible dread, he lifted a corner and exposed a lovely, still face. Tenderly he turned down the bright coverlet and knelt beside his fiancée. One small, bruised hand clung tightly to the edge of the quilt. He called her name, finally shook her in an almost fierce gesture of rebellion, then cradled her body against him only to have her head fall limply back. The girl so soon to have been his bride was dead.

It was 1955 when Dora Monroe and her husband of Kershaw, South Carolina, moved into the handsome old house on Matson Street. A midwestern family had once lived there briefly, then moved; others had come and gone. Dora Monroe was one of those admirable women who pride themselves on meticulous housekeeping and the first thing she did was to give the place a thorough cleaning. When the rooms were painted and the floors refinished and polished to her satisfaction, she decided on the first cool day to straighten the attic. She had left one end of it untouched at the time of the move.

How could there be anything threatening about a quilt?

What a sight it was! There were nuts cached by squirrels, rat droppings, cobwebs hanging from the rafters and crumbling old newspapers along with remnants of broken toys. She was almost through when way back in a dark corner almost hidden under the eves she spied something. It was a large cardboard box and filled with curiosity she tugged it out. A cloud of dust rose as she lifted the lid.

Removing a layer of tissue paper, Dora Monroe was amazed to find one of the most beautiful, handmade quilts she had ever seen. It was well over a hundred years old. A kaleidoscope of colors and in almost perfect condition she immediately visualized it upon her guest room bed.

A few months later, before her daughter Florence Delafosse arrived for the summer, she thought of the quilt and spread it over her bed. Her neighbors, Nancy McCue and Anne Fraser, looked at it with mingled admiration and envy.

Florence arrived to visit her mother the first day of May. After hugging her mother, chatting for awhile, and unpacking only her most needed toilet articles she retired. It was after midnight when she awoke certain that her mother must be pulling the covers up around her shoulders as she had done when Florence was a child. But when she called out, "Mother?" in the darkness, there was no answer and she supposed that her mother had left.

Dozing off, Florence was again awakened, this time by tugging motions on the quilt, and reaching down she attempted to pull it back over her. She was frightened but stubbornly continued to clutch the coverlet and soon it became a tug-of-war in the pitch black bedroom. There was a stronger than usual jerk and she heard the hollow, spectral voice of a woman close to the bed.

"Give me back my quilt. It's my Christmas gift," said the voice. "Give it back now, or you will be sorry!"

Suddenly, she fell back in bed. The tug at the other end had ceased abruptly. Convinced that she had experienced a most extraordinary nightmare owing to fatigue from her trip, she fell into a restless slumber. The following morning the incident seemed too bizarre to relate to her mother.

A few nights later as she lay awake unable to sleep, she thought she felt the quilt move. At first it was imperceptible. Suddenly, there was a convulsive wriggling and it slithered up around her shoulders and neck. Before she could move, the quilt with a whiplike movement threw itself over her face. Panic stricken, Florence leaped from her bed. She turned on the hurricane lamp on the bedside table and settled herself in a chair in the corner of the room. The quilt lay on the bed in a pile where she had thrown it. She soon felt ridiculous. How could there be anything threatening about a blanket? She gradually became drowsy and was almost asleep when the hall clock struck two. Rousing herself, she was ready to return to bed when ever so gently the triangles and squares began to ripple and undulate. As she stared in amazement the quilt crept toward the head of the bed, straightened itself out and covered it as smoothly as if it had never been occupied.

At that moment she heard a soft knock on her bedroom door and she opened it with the grateful thought that it was her mother. Instead Florence saw the tall figure of a man. He wore a straw farmer's hat, and as he reached for her a dank, putrid odor became almost overpowering. From the outstretched arms her terrified gaze traveled upward to the man's face and when she looked under the broad brim of the hat she nearly fainted. The figure standing before her had a face so bruised and discolored that it scarcely appeared human.

Somehow she was able to slam the door and lock it expecting to hear pounding on the other side at any moment. Her heart thudded wildly and the room grew dark around her.

When morning arrived Florence found herself lying across the bed with the quilt neatly folded beside the door. She never slept under it again. Her fear of the quilt's being even in the same house with her became a phobia, and after relating the strange events to her mother she was somewhat relieved. Nevertheless, they both knew they would feel easier when the quilt was out of the house.

What to do with it became something of a problem. Mrs. Monroe preferred to tell herself that her daughter had arrived in an overwrought state and that the more bizarre events in her story were simply imagined. On the other hand, she was too knowledgeable a woman to give the quilt to a friend in a town as small as Kershaw for if . . . and at this point she would not allow herself to think further.

Several times she considered burning the quilt but when she went to the linen closet to take it out, the bright colors almost seemed to glow in the dim light. She was not able to destroy it. One afternoon a young Midwesterner named Alfred Hansen stopped by for a few hours on his way to the South Carolina coast.

The conversation turned to antiques and on an impulse Mrs. Monroe brought out the quilt for him to see. He admired it profusely. She was aware of Florence's agitation. Her face became flushed, her breath quickened, and she left the room. Her mother determined the quilt must go. Hansen was overwhelmed but Mrs. Monroe recalled his helping Florence out of the water when she had ventured too far the summer before. She urged him to accept the quilt.

From the start he had been tempted to give in for he was greatly taken with it and had only protested out of courtesy and suprise. By the time he was ready to leave Mrs. Monroe had prevailed.

Several months later a letter arrived for her. Her face grew pale as she read it. She handed it to Florence

December 24, 1954

Dear Mrs. Monroe:

Since I visited your home some most unusual events have occurred. In fact, had I not recently been checked by a physician, I would be even more concerned over my present illness. The doctor, a new friend of mine, impresses one at first as a tall, gaunt almost rough sort of fellow, but he has been very kind and reassuring.

Under normal circumstances I would most certainly begin this letter by thanking you for your generous gift of the quilt I so admired. At the moment it is difficult for me to do so. Indeed, you may be surprised to learn I have even considered some means of destroying your gift! Now, please do not take offense, for I do not mean that in any ungrateful way.

I have slept with the quilt over my bed almost every night that I am able. Although, sometimes when I awaken in the morning I am weak with fatigue and drenched with perspiration. I am convinced that I often wrestle with it all night long! Does that astound you? A quilt that moves?

Yes, that is what I believe I've seen. I am wondering if it does not have an existence of its own. This probably sounds foolish to you. Of course, I had to describe my quilt to Dr. Gerber and showed it to him. When he saw it all he could say was an admiring, "Ya, it is very beautiful."

The poor man was so enamored of it that I even considered giving it to him. But for some reason, victory over this quilt has become something of an obsession with me and I swear, although it may sound absurd, that I shall come out on top. A little pun, eh!

Well, perhaps, you will bear with my wanderings. I am not feeling well tonight and have just called Dr. Gerber who will be here soon. Actually, I humored the good man telling him that if anything happened to me, my housekeeper has been told that he is to have the quilt. He laughed, saying that my illness was certainly not fatal.

Please forgive the smudge on the paper. As I wrote, the light in my room went out. Now, I have gotten it back on. And, where is the quilt at the moment? It is on my bed, of course, and I have it just over my knees. No, this should prove to you that it *can* move. It is now almost up to my neck. . . . My God!

And there the letter to Mrs. Monroe ended. Enclosed was a brief note.

I am forwarding Hansen's letter to you written just before his attack. Undoubtedly, his hallucinations resulted in the unconscious state in which I found him. At my recommendation he has left for a rest and change of scene. He insisted on giving me his quilt which, pathetically enough, the poor fellow believes to have been a factor in his illness.

Respectfully,
John Gerber

The letters of the signature were tall and flowing. Dora Monroe sat down and wrote to Alfred Hansen. Three months passed and there was still no reply. She decided to phone and discovered Hansen's telephone had been disconnected. On impulse she asked the operator for the number of Dr. John Gerber.

"We have a Hans Gerber and a Eugene Gerber. Could it be one of those?"

"No."

"Well, madam, I'm checking. . . . I don't find that we've ever had a listing for a Dr. John Gerber."

VII

The Blue Lady of Hilton Head

The August hurricane of 1898 was not unexpected. In fact, it had been heralded for at least three days and warnings were given before it made its appearance. The weather bureau found it lurking in West Indian waters. It was gathering itself and taking on ominous threatening form in the Caribbean.

At Hilton Head Island, South Carolina, Adam Fripp knew there was nothing to do except lay in supplies and wait. He had been keeper of the 136-foot lighthouse for three years and a widower for two. His twenty-year-old daughter, Caroline, was as interested in his work as he. She was worried about the danger the storm meant for ships at sea.

The hurricane, after moving west and then to the south, had turned and was heading directly for the South Atlantic coast. Like some evil monster, it seemed to be feeding and gathering strength as it came, thought Caroline, but it might yet go out to sea.

Jeremiah, who helped her father clean the tower, gave his opinion on the likelihood of the storm striking with one of the island sayings.

"June too soon, July stand by, August come it must," and he looked pessimistically at the ocean. This was August. Adam's face was grave as he slipped on his indigo blue uniform and adjusted the summer canvas helmet. Caroline noticed how tired he looked. His face had the grayish tinge it had taken on after a mild heart attack the year before. The long climb up the lighthouse steps can't be good for him, she worried. Nevertheless, he mounted them if anything more quickly than usual. Caroline was just behind him her dark, shiny hair glinting and her dress bright blue in the last rays of the sun that shone through the openings in the metal tower.

Little by little she had begun to share the duties with her father. Every two months she would help wash the lens with wine, and the lamps inside the lens were alternated every fifteen days. She also trimmed the wick and adjusted the lamp. Once she spilled oil on the lens but her father had taught her to pour some wine on her cloth and clean it quickly.

The light, an acetylene torch, sat on a pedestal surrounded by tall glass windows. Caroline felt very important as she worked in her linen apron worn to prevent even the possibility of coarse clothing scratching the lens. The rules were very strict and the keepers were required to have their lens and lantern in order by ten o'clock each morning for lighting in the evening.

The next morning it was raining and the rain continued all day Saturday. Caroline braved the weather to take her father his supper.

"I'm going to spend the night here tonight, Caroline. You go on back to the house."

"Let me put more oil in the lamp father so that it will last all night and then you can come back with me."

"No, it's especially important that we maintain a good light tonight, Caroline." He was proud of that light for its Fresnel lens compared favorably with European lights.

"You go on over to the house and take everything inside that might blow away. Then secure the shutters."

Caroline brought in the wooden rockers and plant stands from the porch. She was relieved that her father had brought home cornmeal, sweet potatoes, turnips and other provisions for it would be a week or more before he would be going to Savannah.

The rain had stopped momentarily, and not yet ready to go back to the lighthouse, she sat on the edge of the porch. Her dog, Frisky, settled himself beside her. Not far from the house was the edge of the forest with its large pines, among

*She was terrified in the darkness, but she felt her
way down counting the rungs.*

them scattered sweet gums and water oaks. It was that time of day the island blacks called the half dark. Stillness hung over the little clearing and the air seemed heavy and stagnant.

Even Frisky seemed to sense the approaching storm. He held up his head and sniffed the air and moved restlessly. Caroline packed food to take over to the lighthouse. Her father would need it during the long night ahead. And then a thought occurred to her. She would stay too.

A sharp gale had sprung up from the northeast. She found her father staring out to sea through his binoculars and wondered what he could see.

"Caroline, there's a ship out there."

"And it's in too close?"

"It's dangerously close if I can see it in this weather."

Adam Fripp had a seaman's eye when it came to judging distances. The weather was worsening and the wind was literally tearing at the tower.

"Do you think a ship can see our light?"

"Optimum visibility for the light is twenty miles. In a storm like this, I wonder if it's a mile. But this is when a ship needs to see that light the most."

"And if there is a break for a moment in the clouds out there. . . ."

"Yes, even visibility for a few seconds could make all the difference."

The storm was getting worse by the minute. It made her think of a raging beast trying to reach its prey. A beast without rule or reason that would hear no pleas for mercy. The wind rattled the window frames and battered at them as if it sought to come in. She saw her father looking at them, too. Neither mentioned it and Caroline unwrapped the sandwiches she had brought. The rain was torrential and the wind continued to gather force.

Caroline looked at the barometer and her face turned white. She had never seen a reading so low and was about to question her father when there was a sound like a sharp explosion followed by glass shattering on the floor. The gale had blown out one of the windows. Her father went into the storage room and came back with several boards but there was no way to hold them over the opening so that he could nail them in place. Another pane shattered explosively and at two minutes before six the light went out.

"The torch! Get the torch!"

Rain was blowing in the two open windows and all was in darkness but Caroline went into the storage room and finally managed to put her hands on the torch. She handed it to her father and he lit the lamp but in a few minutes the wind extinguished it again. Caroline tried to shield it with a board and for two hours her father continued to light the lamp and each time the wind extinguished it.

Caroline was drenched from the rain and she knew her father to be also. The lamp went out and once more she waited to see the hand illuminated by the blow torch reach up to relight it, but nothing happened. Why had he not lighted the lamp as he had done time after time.

"Light the lamp, father," she cried out but there was no answer. She found the torch on its side on the floor, reached for the pedestal and managed to light it. As the glow of the lamp temporarily illuminated the small room, she saw her father lying almost at her feet clutching his chest in agony. He was unable to speak. She was just able to loosen the collar of his shirt beneath the blue uniform coat before the light went out once more.

Scrambling back to where she thought she had left the torch she realized it was gone and for a moment she was filled with panic. Then she remembered that it was still in her hand when she had knelt over her father. Was he going to die right here in the midst of this horrible storm before she could get him home or go for help?

Caroline crawled back through the water on the floor rather than stand and be buffeted by the gusts of rain coming through the two broken windows. When she discovered the torch it was in her father's hand but he had not succeeded in raising himself from the floor to light the lamp. She took it

Out of this window Caroline watched the increasing
fury of the storm.

from him and was able to light the lamp wick although she
wondered how much longer it would remain dry enough to
ignite.

She knew her father should be home in bed but how would
he get down the stairs and walk through the storm to the
house?

"We have to get you home!" She shouted it several times
above the noise of the storm before she could make him understand. Finally, with her arm under his, he began to crawl
little by little toward the door to the lighthouse stairs. But
try as he would, Adam was too unsteady even to crawl down
the steps. There was nothing to do but wait until morning.
Caroline made him as comfortable as she could and urged

him to sleep until the storm had passed. In the morning she could send someone for a doctor on the mainland. Exhausted, she fell into a deep slumber.

When Caroline awoke she had no idea how long she had slept. Outdoors there was no sound of wind or rain. All was quiet. She decided she would go outside and see how much damage had been done by the storm. The inside of the tower was dark as pitch but she felt her way down; by counting the rungs she knew when she was almost at the bottom. She had reached the last dozen steps when her outstretched foot plunged down into water. She drew it back hastily, retreated a few steps and sat down in the darkness to think.

The water was at least two feet deep in the tower. She realized with horror that this meant the water on the island was at least four feet deep and possibly more. What had happened to the cattle and pigs, her own dog Frisky, and to people? The girl shuddered. How long would it be before she could get her father home now that the storm was past? It would be dangerous for him to try to walk to the house through water this high. Somehow, she must summon a doctor.

As she sat there thinking she heard the wind pick up outside. Rain pummeled the metal lighthouse again. The full fury of the storm had returned. Numbed by her predicament she continued to sit on the stair. Suddenly, she was shocked to feel water slosh over her toes. In less than an hour it had risen almost a foot! She lifted her skirt and the sopping wet hem dripped water on her leg. Panic stricken she went back up the stairs and sat near her father. He appeared to be still asleep. Morbid thoughts went through her mind and frightened prayers. Again she fell asleep.

When she awoke it was daylight. The storm had passed and the sky was clear. Caroline looked out one of the broken windows and gasped.

"Father," she cried out. "The island is covered with water!"

Then she remembered that he was still asleep and she must not frighten him.

"I'm not surprised, Caroline," said her father and he attempted to rise. Caroline's strong, young arm half lifted, half steadied him.

"I'm all right," he said protesting her help.

"You're not all right. We need to get a doctor at once."

"And where are you planning to get him?"

"From the mainland. I'll send over there for one."

"Look at that water. It will be two or three days before any help arrives from the mainland."

"Two or three days!"

"At least that."

"Papa, do you see that empty lifeboat floating by?"

"Yes, and over there is someone's house lodged against the tree."

"But the roof is torn off. Whatever happened to the people?"

Her father didn't answer.

"Have you looked at our house?" he asked.

Caroline went quickly to one of the two remaining windows.

"It's there! Thank heaven, Papa. We must try to get home at once."

"You must go ahead, Caroline. I'll come as soon as I get the light cleaned for tonight."

"Then, I'll help and we will go together."

She slipped the linen apron on over her blue dress and worked quickly replacing the wet wick. She noticed that her father's fingers trembled. How would he manage on the stairs? But he did, holding on to the rail as he went. Caroline was close at his side and as they slowly descended the steps she wondered how high the water would be in the bottom of the tower. Unless it had gone down considerably, she was uncertain whether her father would be able to walk to the house. But they started out, his arm over her shoulder and hers about his waist. Now and then he would stop and lean against the rail of the circular metal stairs for his breath was short.

At the bottom of the lighthouse he struggled to open the

door, and between the two of them they were able to swing it slowly open through the water. It was tiring to walk in the water and soon Caroline found that her father was leaning upon her heavily.

"Are you all right, Papa?"

"Yes, Caroline." But even as he spoke pain rippled across his face, and she felt the weight of his body almost more than she could stand up under.

"My legs feel so heavy. I don't know why, daughter. I don't know. . . ." by now her father was staggering slightly. They were about half way to the house.

"Let's stand here a moment and rest," said Caroline.

"No, better that I go on now." His face was gray but he continued to plod unsteadily through the water. What if he falls thought Caroline, her arm aching. Her leg struck something sharp and hard and it hurt so that she cried out.

"Caroline, what's the matter?"

She reached down in the water and pulled up a child's rocker lying just beneath the surface. But where was the child? She heard her father groan and when she looked at his face she knew he was suffering a heart attack. He could scarcely stand. With almost superhuman strength Caroline waded on through the water urging him along, and somehow he was able to remain on his feet. When they were just a short distance from the house she circled his chest with her arms, locked her fingers together, and managed to inch back toward the porch a little at a time.

He was about to sink down into the water and she knew if he did she would never be able to lift him out. There was the sound of cloth ripping. Her father had grasped the skirt of her blue dress in his hand to keep from sliding below the surface of the water. She had almost reached the porch.

As she moved her right foot behind her she felt something firm yet oddly yielding. A horrible thought crossed her mind. It might be a corpse! Then she felt the edge of the porch hard against her back and turning she was able to push the upper part of her father's body over it. After he rested he was able to pull himself up with Caroline's help. The effort so exhausted him that he wanted to rest there and she covered him with a blanket.

All was quiet and it seemed forever before she saw any sign of life. Finally an island fisherman, Donald Stuart, appeared in a small dinghy and Caroline called to him. Together they lifted her father into his bed.

"Mr. Stuart, could you get a doctor?"

He gestured to the boat half filled with water. It had been damaged by the storm and was leaking badly.

"I know your father's mighty sick but I've got to keep lookin' for my two older children. Maybe, somewhere, they're alive. My wife and baby drowned last night," and Stuart went on his way, the dinghy low in the water.

Caroline folded a blanket into a pallet beside her father's bed and after changing the blue dress for dry clothes she slept a troubled sleep filled with nightmares of the house being swept out to sea, struggling to save her father, while all around them in the water, people were crying out for help.

It was late afternoon when she felt the rays of the sun warm upon her face through the window and awakened. How very quiet everything was. She realized that since the storm she had not heard a bird sing.

"Papa, have you seen a bird?"

For a moment there was no reply and then he answered weakly.

"They have all been blown away."

"Blown away? Killed by the storm?"

"No. But it was a mighty wind and it probably blew them inland. They will be back in a few days." His voice was very weak. Caroline built a fire in the wood stove and heated some broth for her father but he wasn't able to drink more than a few mouthfuls.

"You must go over, light the lamp and keep it in my place tonight, Caroline." She nodded. The last rays of the sun shone in through the window upon her father's face. He turned his head away and fell asleep.

She trudged to the tower through the water that had gone down until it was just below her knees. There was no breeze and after she lighted the lamp she decided it was unlikely to go out and that she would go back to the house to be with her father. Near the steps of the lighthouse she saw something yellow in the water and reaching down to tug at it found that it was a doll still clutched by the fingers of a dead child. For a moment she thought she would faint but she recovered herself.

When she went back in her father's bedroom he was lying on his side in the same position he had been when she left. She called but there was no answer. Then she turned his face toward her and looked down at him. Adam Fripp was dead, and the daughter who loved him more than anyone else in the world began to sob uncontrollably. But there was no one to hear and no one to comfort her.

The next morning Stuart was at the door. He had noticed that the light in the lighthouse was out. Stuart and two other islanders returned a few hours later with a wooden sea chest. They weighted it, took it into the ocean, and left it far out beyond the low water mark. "Die by water, lie by water," Stuart had said as they lowered the chest over the side.

One of the women tried to get Caroline to come home with her but she refused to leave the house. Sometimes at night she was seen walking between her home and the lighthouse calling her father. She always seemed to be wearing the long, blue dress she had worn on the night of the hurricane, the dress torn and bedraggled. It was soon apparent she would not survive the shock of the storm and the tragedies following it. A few weeks later Caroline died.

Many a year has passed but now and then on wild and stormy nights, a girl is seen in one of the lighthouse windows or at the foot of it. The folds of her flowing blue dress are sculptured by the wind as she walks near the rusted old tower weeping and wringing her hands.

A young policewoman who patrols this part of the island says, "Sometimes she isn't heard from for years and then the story surfaces again. The Blue Lady is reported most often during hurricane season and I've talked with people who swear they've seen her. Others say they've heard the sound of a woman sobbing not far from where the keeper's house once stood. I only know that I wouldn't go near that old lighthouse on windy, rainy nights."

VIII

The Convivial Spirit of Cool Springs

Charleston is not the only place noted for its ghosts. Shades and apparitions abound in the upcountry where the ghosts of the past and those of the present may even meet!

At Rectory Square Park in the heart of Camden, the dramatic roll of Confederate drums and a blood-curdling rebel yell have been known to pierce the night air. Near Mulberry Plantation a magnificent white stallion gallops among the trees at twilight.

And then there is the story of one of Camden's most haunted plantations. From the blacktop highway a sand road meanders through fragrant pine woods until it reaches a lush, green clearing. In its midst rises an imperious, white-columned home resplendent as a gleaming jewel in a velvet case. It is a perfect setting for a modern-day ghost!

Camden's Cool Springs Plantation house is one of those thirty room-mansions South Carolinians modestly dubbed "Summer Houses" during the 1800s. Here the Boykin family retreated from the heat and humidity of their swampy farm fields some ten miles distant. Their farm was near Wateree Swamp and this house on higher ground was a refuge from the dread country fever. It would be years before the link between mosquitoes and the fever was known.

William and Mary Chesnutt Boykin built this imposing three-story home, designed its magnificent paneling, supervised the carving of the Adams style fireplace by slaves, and decorated the twenty-foot high ceilings with elaborate medallions.

A century and a half later John Bonner and his friend Gaffney Blalock counted themselves fortunate to be able to purchase Cool Springs. Bonner was retiring as Curator of the Rare Book Collection at the University of Georgia. Blalock taught diagnostic medicine at Clemson University. Their task of restoring Cool Springs was more monumental than the two had ever imagined but they are carrying it out with enthusiasm. Modern-day comfort is everywhere although the basic integrity of the house has been preserved.

On the warm autumn evening we visited Cool Springs, my first glimpse of something unusual was the long-stemmed glass of white wine on the top step beside one of the tall, white columns. I learned that it had not been left there accidentally but was a ritual to greet a ghost.

"We just want to let him know he's welcome to attend our party, if he wants to," says Bonner. He speaks of the ghost of the home's former owner in a gentle, warm way as if he were discussing a good friend.

"The man was a bon vivant if every there was one. I've heard he died here in the house and under somewhat unusual circumstances. In fact, it happened back there in the study," said the silver-haired Bonner waving his hand toward the room behind the larger parlor where we sat.

"Poor fellow. He had a severe heart attack. Was in a good deal of pain and his daughter ran to get his medicine. On her way up the stairs she met her stepmother and told her what had happened.

" 'Go to your room and wait,' said Mrs. Boykin. 'I'll get his medicine immediately and call you as soon as he's better.'

"Lois obeyed and waited thinking she would hear her stepmother's footsteps going to her father's bedroom for the medicine but she did not. An almost unbearable quarter of an hour must have passed when she heard her stepmother screaming.

" 'He's dead! Oh, God! My husband is dead!'

"Much to the servant's shock, the girl rushed downstairs and began shouting at her stepmother.

" 'You killed him, you've killed my father! You didn't give him his medicine.'

"Of course, she told her brother and the pair went around

the house crying and accusing their stepmother. His children weren't at the funeral for how could they possibly be allowed to go when they were carrying on so. Of course, the daughter was overwrought and it's inconceivable that the poor lady would do such a heinous thing."

Dr. Bonner frowned and poked the fire.

"It was a very, very sad thing."

Despite that tragedy, much gaiety has always been associated with Cool Springs. It has been the scene of many elaborate balls and before it was purchased by its new owners, the impressive home was rented for weddings. John Bonner and Gaffney Blalock continue the festive traditions of the great house with sumptuous dinner parties and holiday celebrations.

"We had spent the first months taking down and repairing the tall columns around the house and replacing the Doric rings at the top," says Bonner. "When we finished we celebrated. What a spread! Champagne, smoked turkey, Yorkshire pudding, truffles, mincemeat tarts, everything you can think of.

"After dinner our guests proposed a toast and one after the other, they raised their glasses. Among them was a friend from Washington. He interrupted the dinner table conversation and turning to me said, 'I didn't know you had another guest.' I asked him what he meant.

"'I saw a man walk down that hall and he may have gone into the study.'

"'What did he look like?'"

"'A well-dressed sort of fellow. Dark trousers, sport coat and I think an ascot. He had gray hair and a very pleasant face.'

"'I really don't know who you could mean.'"

A few minutes later the guest had signaled and nodded meaningfully toward the door. Mystified, Bonner arose to look for himself and his guest followed. They walked up and down the hall but no one was there. They even went out on the porch. Dr. Bonner happened to glance over near the pillar

*A glass of wine is sometimes left out to welcome the
ghost of a former owner of Cool Springs.*

where he had left his wine glass. He knew he had left a full
glass behind him when the first guest came. Now, it was
empty. Had it been sampled by the unknown visitor?

They went back into the house and decided to check the
parlor. Bonner switched on the light but no one was there.
The two walked back into the study. Here a lamp was on and
there was the cheerful sound of music. As they stood looking around the room, the music stopped. Then another number began. It was a nostalgic piece from the past and must
have been heard at many a party in this house thought
Bonner.

A sensitive person, he began to experience a strange sensation. It was as if he had left his own party and found another
going on in the same house at the same time. Behind the
notes of the music one could almost imagine the sound of
voices and distant laughter.

He recalled that his friend's description of the uninvited guest was of a man whose clothes were not quite right for the 1980s but more common a few decades ago. In fact, the period when this music they were listening to was popular.

"Where do you think he could have gone?" His guest spoke almost in a whisper.

"I don't really know," Bonner replied. He decided he would turn off the music but as he took a step toward the record player, the melody stopped and all was quiet. He felt the position of the switch.

"This switch isn't even on. It must be the one in the other room." But the switch in the parlor was off, too. In bewilderment, they rejoined the other guests.

The next day Bonner called a good friend who had often visited Cool Springs in the past. He described the appearance of the stranger and said, "Mac, I'm extremely curious as to who that man was. Does my description help?"

"Of course it does. The man who was seen in your house was Dixie Boykin who used to live there. I'd know him anywhere."

"Dixie Boykin?"

"Yes. His wife had lost two husbands and he was her third who died an accidental death."

"What sort of man was Dixie?"

"Well, you might say he liked to live it up, surround himself with friends and play the perfect host."

An afternoon or so later, Bonner, a patrician in his taste and a man who also has the reputation of being a fine host was returning his Steuben crystal to the cupboard when he heard the sound of someone humming. It seemed to come from the dining room. He knew the tune was familiar and then he recalled it. "Lady of Spain, I adore you. . . ." That was it and on it went. It didn't sound like Gaffney but it had to be. Suddenly the humming ceased and at that moment he realized Gaffney was out of town. Could it have been Dixie humming one of his favorites?

Are the owners of Cool Springs afraid of their resident ghost? On the contrary, they have an affection for him.

"He seems to think that the parties we have are for him, too. I wouldn't have it any other way," says Bonner graciously.

"We always pour an extra glass of wine so Dixie will know he is welcome to join us."

IX

The Apparition at Anderson College

In the darkness of the early morning hours doors open noisily and then slam closed at Pitt High School in Greenville, North Carolina. The rhythmic sound of a basketball is heard striking the backboard but the gym is locked and empty. It is said that this high school was built over an early cemetery. At Beloit College in Wisconsin, there are stories of eerie appearances and at Belmont Abbey in Belmont, North Carolina, one of the dormitories is supposedly haunted by the ghost of a murdered nun. South Carolina schools are not immune from these rumors.

A story in the December 19, 1982, issue of the Anderson *Independent Mail* reports some highly unusual happenings at Sullivan Music Center on the campus of Anderson College. This graceful, white-columned building was once the home of a succession of college presidents.

There are conflicting stories about the likelihood of any supernatural events at Sullivan, but one is so absorbing the reader will at least want to hear it. To preserve his privacy from possible administrative probings, we will call the young man involved Hedgepeth.

A few days before all of the excitement reported in the newspaper, Richard Hedgepeth decided to drop by Sullivan on the off chance his roommate was there practicing. Thinking they might go somewhere off campus for supper, he entered the center and immediately heard the sound of a piano in one of the rooms. He opened the door.

The room was illuminated only by the late afternoon light and Hedgepeth was startled to see at the piano, the diaphanous, almost luminous figure of a girl. He managed to blurt out, "Who are you?" and much to his amazement the vaporous figure answered.

"I am Anna, of course."

"What do you mean 'of course?'"

"Everyone knows me because of my father."

"Your father?"

"Yes, don't you know who he is?"

"No."

"Papa is president of this school, stupid!"

"I see. And why do you haunt this building?"

"I am not free to do otherwise, unless I really wanted to, I guess."

"Why aren't you free?"

"I must go on searching."

"Searching for whom?"

When he asked that question the apparition rested a misty but nicely rounded arm on the edge of the piano and bowed her head.

"I don't want to talk about it any more."

The thought occurred to him that she might disappear and he pressed for more information.

"If you will tell me, perhaps I can help you," he said cajolingly. He hadn't the slightest idea just how, but he was determined to find out more.

She lifted her head and seemed to brighten.

"How?"

"First I must know whom you are searching for."

"For him," said the ghost calmly. Richard remained uncomfortably aware that he was not talking with a living person for the communications from the spirit were wordless, its thoughts entering his own mind silently but with perfect clarity.

"And who is 'him?'"

"My fiancé."

"Well, what would you like for me to do?"

"You could make my parents let me see him."

The Sullivan Music Center at Anderson College, where it is said, "Nothing tragic has ever happened on this campus or in the music building."

"Why won't they?"

"They say I'm too young to be engaged."

"How old are you?"

"I'm sixteen and I told them they must let me marry him or I would kill myself! But I didn't really mean to."

"It seems you did. Are you sorry, Anna?"

"Sometimes." She gave a sigh.

"Were there any reasons beside your age?"

"He was Catholic and father didn't like that at all."

"Was he handsome?"

"Francis? Oh, yes. He had blue eyes, curly black hair and the fairest skin. Very much like the young man who comes here in the late afternoon and plays the piano."

"Who is he?"

"How should I know. He plays the most beautiful Strauss waltzes."

"Can you remember one of them," he asked.

She began to sing softly. It was a song about a widow. The music floated through the air and was so distinct he turned toward the door to see if someone else had entered the room. But they were alone. The song broke off in mid-phrase.

"You must promise to help me. If you don't, I'll misbehave!"

"Misbehave? What are you going to do?"

"You wait and see!" There was mischievous laughter like a succession of silvery chimes. The girl's figure faded and soon she had completely vanished leaving the piano bench empty. He stood for a moment in amazement.

When Richard had entered Sullivan the beautiful, glowing afternoon light was turning the panes of the windows gold and making bright pathways on the floor. As he walked out between the tall white columns of the Music Center, it was almost dark.

When he reached the dorm he found his roommate, Frank Ward, reading.

"Frank, you've been over at Sullivan pretty often lately, haven't you?"

"Yes."

"Have you ever seen anything unusual?"

"No. What do you mean?"

"No ghosts or anything?"

"Why would I see ghosts?"

"I don't know. I was really just kidding, I guess."

"That's good. It makes me feel better about you."

"What do you play when you're over there?"

Frank's blue eyes darkened with grief. He frowned slightly and ran his fingers through his curly black hair.

"Richard, dad was a music student here. Since his death I get a feeling of closeness to him when I play some of his favorites."

"Do you ever play Strauss Waltzes?"

At that moment there was a knock on the door and a friend of Frank's came in. They eventually left to study together and Richard's question went unanswered. But it remained in his mind.

The next morning as the two young men walked across the campus together to their first period class, Richard was amazed to see Donnie Martin, one of the maintenance workers, dash out of Sullivan Music Center as if pursued by Darth Vader.

"What's the matter?"

Martin was followed by another maintenance man, Ernie Edwards, who appeared to be as agitated as Martin.

"There's something strange in that place," said Martin.

"There sure is. I heard that music get louder and louder."

"What music?" But Richard was reasonably sure he knew.

"The piano and someone singing."

"What were they singing?"

"I didn't stay around to find out!"

"The closer we got the louder the music was," added Edwards, "So we went the other way. My heart can't take much of that," and he shook his head.

"Come on, Donnie. Let's get a cup of coffee," and off they went.

Frank looked bewildered and Richard thought of what the girl had said about misbehaving. Was she carrying out her threat?

"Let's go in the Center and see who else we can find to talk to," said Richard. The first person they saw was Jim Staggs busily polishing the window panes.

"Have you ever heard anything in here?" asked Richard.

"Not too much unless you count one morning about nine o'clock when I was alone and I heard somebody walking around upstairs. The sound of those footsteps was plain as could be. I went up there and checked all over the place. No one was there but whatever it was had cut on a faucet full blast because the water was running."

"Well, I guess that's about it." Staggs picked up his pail and cloths and off he went. The two young men followed him out of the building where they stood under the large oak just in front of the building.

"What music do you play when you stop off here in the afternoon, Frank?"

"Oh, I don't know. Why?"

"Any Strauss?"

"Yes, I'm reading a book on him right now. Why are you interested?"

"Because I think that's what I heard her playing."

"Heard who playing? You're losing your cool, man."

Richard hesitated to tell his story and Frank was silent for a moment. He seemed to be struggling to recall something.

"Richard, you know how your mom or dad sometimes talk about someone they used to date or who was in love with them?"

"Yeah. It's kind of embarrassing isn't it."

"Once in awhile when dad was feeling down, he would reminisce about a girl he fell in love with while he was in school here. I think he really went for her and wanted to marry her. She was the daughter of the college president. Of course, that was before he met mom and he never mentions it around her."

"Why didn't he marry the girl here?"

"Back then there was a lot of prejudice in the South toward Catholics, and her father didn't even want her to see dad at all."

"So, what happened?"

"She committed suicide."

"Good Lord!"

"Dad thinks she only meant to scare her father but it didn't work out that way. She died."

"That was really bad." There was the sound of the front door of Sullivan closing and they looked up to see maintenance director, Olin Padgett, coming down the steps.

"I want to speak to him a minute, Frank. Wait for me."

"Sure."

"Olin, tell me what's going on inside Sullivan."

Padgett looked a little angry.

"You want me to get in trouble, Richard?"

"What do you mean?"

"Oh, you know. The school's image and all that. Some people would rather I didn't talk about it at all."

"Hold it, Olin. I think a girl really did commit suicide here. Frank's dad knew her." By now they had followed Olin along the side of the building.

"Olin, let's go inside and talk for just a minute."

"All right, all right."

"You've heard walking on the steps in here, haven't you?"

"I didn't pay any attention to the walking up and down those steps until someone else told me they had heard it," said Padgett.

"And what did you say?"

"I told them I'd heard it, too."

"What do you think it is?" asked Frank.

"A benign ghost."

"You really believe there's a ghost in here, Olin?" asked Frank.

"I think there's definitely a presence or a force, whatever you want to call it, that lives in this music building."

At that moment they heard a thunderous chord that seemed to come from the piano in the room across the hall. They all rushed over to it. The room was empty. Frank quickly put his fingers on the keys positioning them.

"Hey, I know that chord, Richard."

He lifted his fingers and came down hard upon the keys. The reverberating notes were followed by a sharp crash.

"Ouch!," cried out Frank for the lid behind the keys had fallen upon his fingers. He removed his hands and shook them making a face as he did so.

"Wasn't that the chord, Richard?"

"That is the one we heard in the other room, all right." The two young men looked at each other incredulously.

Frank never went back again to play at Sullivan but Richard has returned several times. He is insatiably curious about the apparition although he hasn't seen the girl again. But both young men are convinced that "someone" was there.

One caveat, if you should ask the administration at Anderson College about the ghost in Sullivan Music Center you will not find them eager to discuss the matter. Nor do the maintenance men wish to talk about it, and there is no one who will admit to having heard of the suicide of a college president's daughter. In fact, the authoritative word from the college Vice President and Academic Dean, Paul Talmadge, is that, "Nothing tragic has ever happened on this campus or in the music building."

We leave it to our readers and to future generations of students to judge whether the ghost of a lovely girl does or has ever haunted Sullivan Music Center.

X

The Gray Man

Jacqueline Ashley arrived at Pawleys Island in the early afternoon. She had left her Charleston office and without stopping for lunch she had driven to the old house her parents had owned as long as she remembered. There was always something in the refrigerator to make herself a sandwich. She found some mayonnaise, bread in the freezer and a can of chicken.

She had slipped on blue jeans and shed her shoes and now she sat at the kitchen table looking like a teen-ager. Her long brown hair was loosened from its sophisticated knot and lay bouncy and free down her back. Often she met her parents here but she never hesitated to stay at the house alone even in October when most families had left. She considered it the safest place in the world.

It was where she liked to come and think, and when she walked along the beach in the early morning or late afternoon, she had always been able to sort things out and see what was really important in life.

Jacqueline wanted to extend these next few days—make them last a long time. She decided the best way was to be very lazy. She curled up in a chair with a novel, and without intending to, fell asleep like a child. It was over an hour before she awakened.

Then, opening the large wardrobe with the sweaters and jackets in it, she put on a bright red windbreaker and a few minutes later felt the hard wet sand near the edge of the surf beneath her feet. The wind off the water blew her hair and the salt spray settled on her face and clothing like a fine mist.

For the past few years she had thought that the more accomplishments she crowded into her life, the more she would enjoy it. Days raced past and she couldn't think of anything she had really done that gave her satisfaction. Or they dragged by as if they would never end. Only now and then did tempo and meaning come together. Here at Pawleys she would find the answer.

She passed a surf fisherman on the beach, a man she knew slightly, and nodded. Before she knew it she had reached the end of the island and she retraced her steps rather than walk back on the creek side. The light was fading quickly now. The wind was higher and she had begun to feel the chill, but still she did not hurry.

Once she stooped to pick up a shell and looked back. Whether she saw the figure walking along the beach then or became aware of it later when she climbed a dune and stared out over the ocean she could not remember afterward. She was still some distance from the house when she realized she was being followed.

She would walk for awhile, then steal a look over her shoulder and he would still be two or three hundred feet behind her. She could not recall ever having seen him before although she knew most of the people on the island. He was a stranger and something about him sent a cold chill down her back. Perhaps he would turn off at one of the beach houses. He did not. She paused thinking he might sense her apprehension, for they were the only two people on the beach, and pause himself. But he did not.

On he came, as relentlessly as a robot, thought Jackie. I could run and see what happens. But the consequences of running, being pursued and perhaps caught on the desolate winter beach struck sudden fear in her heart. She hastened her pace and as she glanced back she noticed that the man, too, was walking faster.

*She would walk for awhile, then steal a look over her shoulder
and he would still be two or three hundred feet behind her.*

Jackie's heart began to pound wildly. The comforting and
familiar had turned to the strange and terrifying. What would
she do when he caught up with her as he surely would? She
could turn toward an opening in the dunes and race toward
someone's home but most houses were empty this time of
year. Where was the fisherman she had seen? Hadn't he been
down opposite the Pelican Inn? No, he was gone.

Her breath began to come faster but to her great surprise,
when she looked back again, she saw her unknown pursuer
standing on top of a dune looking toward the sea. It was getting dark. Mist was rolling in from the ocean and even as she

watched, a great gust of mist borne on the wind enveloped and swallowed him. Jacqueline ran as fast as she had ever run.

An hour later as she warmed herself before the small heater in the kitchen, it seemed ridiculous that anyone had followed her on the beach. That night she slept a troubled, fitful sleep. Whether it was because of her experience that afternoon, the sound of the wind or the increasingly heavy rain, she could not be sure. She woke about two o'clock, decided to check the window locks, and fell asleep until five when she awoke thinking she had heard footsteps on the porch outside her windows. She went to one of the tall, old fashion windows and pulled back the curtain to look out. By the porch light she could see heavy gusts of rain and the old house seemed to groan and shudder from the force of the wind. She was sure it was no ordinary storm but surely if a hurricane was on the way there would have been radio warnings. She went back to sleep.

Out on the lonely beach it was that last hour before the sun comes up. Not today, but most days the sun would rise and the rim of the world far away where the water ended would be suffused with a rosy red. Then the sky would lighten as if the curtains of the world were opening for another act. For the man walking the beach, this island was his world and he loved it.

In the early years it bothered him that even on the brightest of summer days, he could never seem to see his shadow on the sand. It wasn't really important except that it was part of that keen perception of self he had felt at first. There had been vivid memories of family, the taste of foods, voices he loved; and sometimes when he was especially lucky, the way her face had felt beneath his finger tips as he touched it gently.

Later it was a struggle to recall events and people. So much eluded him now except for the sense of his mission and that was still strong within him year after year. It was a magnet drawing him toward the houses and out of them he would choose just one. To him, it was as if that house belonged to his sweetheart of long ago although in a dim sort of way, he really knew it did not. He would single out that house, knock and after he had performed his task, go back from whence he had come.

At the moment he was aware of the sea oats bent almost to the ground, sand blowing in the wind and the dark foaming water. It was going to be one of the worst, he thought as he looked toward the sea. She would be at her wildest and most savage soon. With a sense of urgency he walked toward the houses behind the dunes. He remembered the girl in the bright red jacket he had watched walking on the beach the afternoon before. Where had she gone? What house did she live in?

Now, he was beginning to live, to feel elated just as he always did when a storm was on the way. From a distance there was an almost youthful look to him as he strode along beside the pounding surf. For a brief moment he thought about a time long, long ago. About a race and his horse falling under him. He recalled wet, devouring sand all around him. There was a vague sense of horror before the scene faded and mercifully he remembered no more.

He stood upon one of the dunes in the driving rain trying to decide which house belonged to the girl in the red jacket. Suddenly, he was sure. His uncanny sense of direction was working. He would find her. Clouds of rain and wind borne mist billowed about him as he strode along with a steady, purposeful gait.

Jacqueline, awakened by the howling of the wind, lay wide-eyes in the darkness listening to the fury of the storm. She was not frightened for she had been through many storms on the island. Rather, she was thinking about the man on the beach. Who was he? Why did he seem to be following her? For the first time she wished that her family was here.

The noises of the old house grew greater in response to the mounting wind and the pounding surf was a dark obbligato to the clattering shutters and air whistling through the cracks

---

around the windows. Beach houses were never built to be tight and the wind explored every crevice. She recalled the time her father had urged the family out of the house one afternoon in a storm, how the bushes had lashed at their bare legs and arms as they raced for the car. And then the drive to the mainland in a torrential rain. Surely, it would be better just to stay on the island.

Of course, like others with homes on the coastal islands, Jackie had heard stories of flooding to the second floor and of some houses swept into the ocean. The porch swing was striking the house with a bang, bang, bang! It was a sign of the force of the wind and she parted the curtain to look out. Gradually she became aware of more. The cloud of mist beneath the porch lamp was taking on a solid appearance. It was the outline of a man!

Her heart gave a lurch and she felt faint. Then came a pounding on the front door that could be heard above the roar of the storm. Her first thought was not to go. The pounding continued. There was a long silence and she breathed a deep sigh of relief. He had gone. Jackie decided she would wait until daylight before making up her mind to leave.

She was back in bed when she heard a sharp rap on her window pane. The rapping was so insistent that Jackie threw her robe on and cautiously inched open the front door. There stood the man she had expected to see. The man who had followed her on the beach. A gray cloud of mist swirled up around him.

"You must leave the island immediately. A severe storm is going to strike soon," said a voice out of the clouds of vapor. Jackie was too frightened to reply.

"Do you hear me? It's important that you leave right away!"

"Yes, yes. I hear you and I'll leave now," Jackie heard herself saying.

Wind blew the umbrella from her hands and by the time she reached the car, she was drenched. Brushing wet hair back from her eyes, she strained to see through the sheet of rain over her windshield. Were there other cars on the road to the mainland? She was not even sure she would see their lights in this downpour. Her shoulders and arms were tense as she steered carefully, hoping to stay in the right lane. Something large and black swept across the road in front of her—a broken off tree top. Finally she reached her apartment in Charleston safely, stripped off her damp clothing, and fell asleep exhausted.

When she awoke late that afternoon all of Charleston was talking about the hurricane. Gracie, as they called it, had cut a wide swath of devastation along the coast. Jackie thought of the man on the island who had warned her, probably sent by the Civil Defense or other authorities. Now her fear of him seemed foolish.

Sitting in the swing on the front porch of the undamaged house a week later, she thought about the warning. By now she had talked with everyone who had been on the island that day—only a few people actually, owing to the season. She had also questioned authorities who had closed the causeway. No one knew of any warning, and some said, it had to be the Gray Man, a story she had always thought was just island folklore.

Two hundred years ago a young man was returning to his fiancée after a journey. Not far from her home his horse fell and both horse and rider died in the treacherous quick sand. The ghost of the young man returned to warn his sweetheart of an approaching storm and from then on, over the years, there were amazing reports of a stranger who would warn a family on the island before particularly savage storms. Jackie, the down-to-earth daughter of a Georgetown businessman, had always considered the story more fancy than fact.

Now, she recalled the strangeness she had felt about that figure that had followed her along the beach, the way he had seemed to vanish from the top of the sand dune. She could not even recall the face of the man surrounded by swirling, gray mist who had spoken to her when she opened the door. Her skepticism wavered, flickered like a candle flame in the wind and was gone. Jacqueline Ashley was sure that she had seen the Gray Man.

XI

Danger House

It was ten at night when the phone in the Charleston motel room jangled and a man's voice on the other end of the line said, "You may be the only person who will understand when I tell this story." I had been waiting for his call.

That morning I had braved hurricane-like rain to reach the downtown Post Office and find out whether my newspaper advertisement had produced results. It read, "If you have ever encountered a ghost or had an experience you believe was supernatural, please write at once. This information is for a university press publication."

I had run the ad for a week and driven to Charleston to interview the writers of the replies I hoped to receive. But what if no one had answered? Where would I look next for modern day ghost stories? To my great relief, the box was half full of letters! Some replies contained episodes that appeared to be supernatural but were fragmentary. Several had excited my interest, particularly, one in a white envelope with the name Browder printed in dark blue. The address was James Island.

Paul Browder began his story by telling me that he and his wife had spent their vacations in South Carolina for several years before deciding that it was the ideal place for "two Yankees like ourselves" to retire. An important part of their dream was to buy an old Southern home. Of course, it must have columns, perhaps a balcony, and some fascinating history to impress their Northern friends.

"Eight years ago we found just the place we wanted out here on James Island. It wasn't quite in the state of repair we had hoped for but it was two hundred years old and had history bursting out of the seams. We were told it had once been headquarters for Confederates and that Jefferson Davis had stayed there. Others said the ghosts of slaves had been seen and even heard in the rooms and on the stairs. We've never believed in ghosts but we thought that really added spice. I bought it.

"I remember telling Maggie, 'Tomorrow we go back to Baltimore to our row house and start packing. We've brought up all the kids and it's been fine. But now we're really going to live the good life. You can tell your sister, Bridget, that your new home is a house where Jeff Davis once stayed.'

"Maggie laughed and said, 'Bridget and her husband, O'Malley, never heard of Jeff Davis.' She was right. I've always been one of those Civil War buffs myself.

"Well, we moved into the old Clark house in late June. It was on Targave Street in Clark's point subdivision. There were four big rooms downstairs and four upstairs. We couldn't believe we were living in a house that size at first.

"What I'm getting to now sounds pretty far out, so it's a good time for me to say that I was Police Chief of Baltimore for over twenty-five years and anybody who knew me knew I was a down to earth man. I saw plenty in a big city, mostly just human meanness though; nothing that couldn't be explained. But from the time we first moved in, Maggie and I noticed weird things about that house—doors opening and closing, objects in crazy places, and noises. Good Lord!

"One night we came in about midnight and were upstairs in bed watching a television movie. All of a sudden we heard a terrible racket in the kitchen. It sounded like every dish in our cupboard was tumbling to the floor and smashing to bits. Maggie and I jumped out of bed and ran downstairs. When we got to the door and looked in, I couldn't believe it. There wasn't a dish on the floor and the kitchen was as neat and clean as a nun's collar. Somehow, that was worse than if we had found it in a shambles.

"Maggie and I looked at each other. She still looks just like

A decaying mansion that was never to find a Yankee restorer.

a little kid when she gets scared. At that moment, I'll admit, I could feel the hair rise on the back of my neck. I tried to act like the tough cop I always thought I was and I told her it was just noise from outside. But that noise wasn't outside, it was right in the house with us.

"It wasn't a week later that we had gone to bed and were lying there in the dark when I heard footsteps coming up the stairs. They weren't like someone trying to sneak up as a thief would do. These were heavy men's steps, the feet slowly shuffling up a step at a time. I looked over at Maggie to say something but she was asleep. The footsteps came on and at the top of the stairs, almost outside our door, they stopped.

"I lay as still as if I were carved out of ice. Finally, they passed on beyond our door and headed toward the front room. I heard the switch click and as it did the darkness in the hall was broken by a path of light that shone through the open guest room door. My heart was trying to beat its way out of my chest.

"An inch at a time I eased open the drawer of the bedside table and pulled out my revolver. Then stood in the hall for a moment. It was so quiet I could hear Maggie's breathing back in the bedroom. As I stood there, the light in the guest room went off.

"I thought of whether I should go in there in the dark. Whoever it was, he was trapped. He couldn't drop from a second story window. Then there was the shuffling sound. I had nothing to decide. He was coming back.

"My hand fumbled for the light at the top of the stairs and flipped the switch but it didn't work. On the footsteps came until they passed me and started down the stairs. As they reached the bottom the light in the upstairs hall came on, just as if someone had touched the downstairs switch. But the hall below was empty. That is not the only time I heard the steps on the stairs but I didn't tell Maggie, although I thought she knew some things about the house she was not mentioning.

"One night we were eating in the kitchen and smoke began to seep out of a crack in the wall behind me. In a moment it was in flames. Luckily, I managed to put it out with a fire extinguisher we kept near the stove.

" 'Sometimes the wiring is bad in old houses,' Maggie said, so next day we had an electrician come.

" 'You have a burned place here but the wiring, as far inside as I can see it, is brand new,' he told us shaking his head.

"Summer passed and one September evening I was sitting on the front porch with a friend named Dobbs who lives nearby. He talked about seeing the shadowy figure of an old lady rocking back and forth on the porch.

" 'It always looked like it might be old Mrs. Clark,' he said. I don't know what made me do it, but I shot back, 'Well, that's better than seeing the Devil!' As I spoke the wall next to us exploded in a burst of flames! I decided right then that I was going to sell that house if I could stay alive long enough to do it, and I did."

I thanked the gentleman for calling and asked if I might see the house.

"I wish you could," he said "but a few weeks after we sold it, the old Clark place burned to the ground."

XII

The Specter of the Slaughter Yards

If a man named Willie Earle could walk the streets of Greenville today, he would feel at home. The city has acquired a scattering of skyscrapers, but many signs of the past remain.

The dirty, cream-colored brick buildings are still common. The old railroad station, an abandoned red monstrosity, dreams on of past grandeur. Families continue to crowd around the tall, white columns of Augusta Heights Baptist Church on Sunday morning. And on each side of Augusta Street, gabled brick and frame homes recall the architecture of the 1920s.

Behind the hill near Wakefield Street nest myriad, monotonous mill houses, a reminder that much of Greenville's work force is still employed in textiles—an industry that sometimes becomes an economic refuge for the uneducated, unskilled and intolerant and bigoted.

This was the setting for a fearful story which was covered by *Life* magazine and the national press. The horror, hurt and haunting have not yet been laid to rest.

It was after midnight when the Yellow Cab dispatcher got a call from the Bramlett Road area. Cab driver Bill McAllister hesitated before saying he would take it. He had seen the eyes of some of the drivers when they had come back from that part of Greenville late at night. He drove on West Washington with Textile Hall coming up on his right. McAllister then turned left at the school and followed Bramlett until it became Blue Ridge.

Once he thought he saw something in the road just in

Now a museum, the jail at Pickens resembled a grim, old fortress. In the hours of early morning, jailer Ed Gilstrap slept peacefully.

front of him and he slammed on the brakes only to see it was just a night animal, maybe a possum. Then he picked up Bramlett Road again. He knew well where he was.

This was the place where the old slaughter yards had been. On his right was an empty field and on the left a development of small, brick ranch houses. His instructions had been to pull over and stop in front of one of the houses on his left, flick the headlights and wait for a passenger. At the first house he began to count until he reached the right one.

Pulling off on the shoulder he felt the cab give a bump and a lurch as if he had run over a large piece of stovewood. What was it? Why was he so nervous? He slowed to a stop, flicked his lights and waited. Who in heaven was he waiting for?

The man's name had only been a mumble over the phone. The house looked dark as pitch.

He decided to get out of the car and have a cigarette. As he tried to strike the match his hand shook. He thought he heard a noise and turned quickly. Was it his passenger? Frogs croaking, nothing but frogs he told himself, but his body was tense. Then he heard it again and it was not frogs. It was a low, gutteral moan carried by the wind.

The moan was unmistakable. It was the voice of a man in pain and he could hear the words, "I swear, it wasn't me! I don't know who did it. Aaaah!" The scream swelled into a horrifying crescendo, and it seemed the cry of agony would go on in the night forever.

Every thought left McAllister save overwhelming fear. Desperately he reached for the handle of the cab door but failed to find it, and even as he groped for it, the darkness near him seemed to take shape and move. McAllister shook with fear and it was all he could do to keep from leaving his cab and running.

There was the whomp, whomp, whomp of heavy sticks striking with a thud, the sound of ripping fabric and another scream split the night wide open like a razor sharp switchblade cutting through human flesh.

"Lord, you done killed me!" he heard a man's voice cry. Then there was a shout. "Give me the gun. Let's get it over with!" Shots rang out.

At that moment McAllister's fingers found the door handle. He dived into the cab, slammed it in gear and spun the car around on the road but there was something standing in the road blocking his path. The car headlights illuminated an indescribably frightful and grisly sight.

"God!," exclaimed the cabbie swerving the car, and with his foot pressed to the floorboard he took off. When he walked into the Yellow Cab office thirty minutes later the dispatcher stared curiously.

"Look like you might be going to get sick, fellow. Did you pick up your passenger?"

"I didn't wait, Curton, I'm never going to pick up a passenger out that way after dark again. Lord, the poor bastard! Maybe I'm going crazy."

"You're not going crazy, Bill. I'd be willing to bet you've seen the same thing some of the other drivers have and it's bad."

McAllister groaned, his face in his hands.

"Don't know when I've been that scared. What in the name of heaven was it and why did I see it?"

"Because you're a cab driver, that's one reason."

"What are you talking about!"

"There's only one guy left that could tell you all about it and then you might be sorry you asked. It all happened thirty-five years ago."

Dick Curton shook his head as if memories could be cast off or shrugged away like an unwanted hand on the shoulder.

"He's a cold one, Johnny is. Always was but for some reason he trusted me. Putting together what he said and the stories I read in the papers, I'll tell you as much as I know of the whole thing. I'm going to start with something that happened back in 1944.

"One of our drivers, Johnny Worthington, was cruising along Main Street one spring afternoon when he saw a tall man in a tan raincoat standing under a drugstore awning. The man signaled and he pulled over. The fellow had lived up North and he was black. Worthington despised blacks and particularly the ones that had lived up North for awhile.

"'Nice raincoat you've got,' Johnny said to his passenger. The fellow mumbled something and Johnny went on talking.

"'Yeah, wouldn't mind having me one like that but it's bound to look better on a big, strapping fellow like you. Hey, I gotta mind to try it on. Whatcha say, boy?'

"'That wouldn't bother me none.'

"'Wouldn't bother you? Well, how 'bout that, 'cause it would sure bother the hell outa me. I might take it off and find some of that black had rubbed off on me!' The man on the back seat wouldn't answer, just kept looking out the

This is the same key that Gilstrap used to open the jail door on the morning of February 17, 1947.

window. Johnny was taking him out the Laurens Road to his mother's place and while they drove he went on baiting him.

"'They got shed of you up North and you've come back down here, right? I hear whites and blacks eat in the same restaurants together up there. Is that true, boy?' I don't think the man answered him back.

"Knowing Worthington, he probably was laughing that nervous little laugh of his that always came between the things he said. Sometimes it got under your skin because he did it whether something was serious or not. Just a habit.

"Pretty soon they were there. A neat little white bungalow set back about a hundred yards from the highway. As Johnny told it, the house looked right pretty in the late afternoon sunlight with tall, pink cleome in bloom on either side of the dirt road leading up to it. He reached back and opened the door for his passenger. He wasn't about to take the fellow to the house. Johnny was too mean for that.

"The guy got out and began to stride across the black top toward the sand road. Worthington called out, 'Hey, you ain't paid me yet.'

"'Why, you son of a bitch,' the black man replied. 'I'd like to break your neck.'

"He turned and went on walking toward the house. Johnny reached down, pulled out a pistol, aimed it and squeezed the trigger. There was a sharp crack followed by a second and a third. The man fell to his knees. His arms jerked upward toward the sky almost like he was praying and then he toppled over face down in the road.

"When he told me a little about it the next morning, it was more like he was asking me a question and then letting me draw my own conclusion.

"'Haven't read anything about a black getting shot have you, Curton?' At first I say, no, and he laughs that little laugh of his. Then I see a story way down at the bottom of a page, something about a body being found out on Laurens Road, a black man shot three times in the back.

"'Well, that's one less of 'em,' said Johnny with a smirk, those pale blue eyes of his cold as ice. It wasn't till a month or so later he told me all about it.

"Of course, this was back before Brown was stabbed to death in his cab one night and all hell broke loose. It turned my stomach then and still does even though it happened back in February of 1947. There was a black man arrested for the killing and his name was Willie Earle. I was in the court room listening the day his mother Tessie was testifying.

"According to Tessie Earle it was Saturday night, February 15, when she heard the Greyhound bus stop not far from Reid's Restaurant where she worked. She was suprised because that bus usually went right through Liberty without stopping. When she got home there sat her son Willie down from Virginia.

"Willie said he was sick with a cold and his momma said, 'Boy, have you just come home 'cause you're sick.' He laughed because he knew she was glad to see him. He was the oldest of her seven children. She was only fourteen when Willie was born. Now, he was twenty-three, maybe, a little stocky and about medium height. Sometimes he had a problem with epilepsy but not the way he used to when he was a boy. He liked to work outdoors and had a broad smile that sometimes turned into a belly laugh.

"His baby sister asked him for money for Sunday School and Willie told her he didn't have none, nothin' but two dollars and he'd give her one of them in the morning. She tried to get in his pocket and he pulled out his wallet and showed her the two dollar bills.

"When Tessie Earle got up Sunday morning she fixed a big pancake breakfast for everybody and left to go to the restaurant. Two of Willie's friends had dropped by and they were talking and listening to the radio. When Tessie Earle finished up at the restaurant about two o'clock and walked out the door two policemen stood waiting to talk to her.

" 'We caught your boy, Willie,' they told her.

" 'Caught him! What are you talking about? He's at home.'

" 'That's where we got him, Tessie. Your boy robbed and cut up a cab driver bad. We took Willie by the hospital and the driver woke up for a few minutes and said he did it.'

" 'Lord, Willie didn't come home in a cab, he came on the bus. I heard that bus stop and let him off. You know it doesn't usually stop at Liberty."

"That night she and the two oldest children went to the jail in Pickens.

" 'Which Earle are you wanting to see?' asked jailer, Ed Gilstrap.

" 'How many do you have in here?'

" 'A fellow named James Earle is here. They brought him in drunk as a coot.'

" 'No, sir. My son is Willie Earle and they're accusin' him of something he didn't do.'

"That same night in Greenville angry cab drivers were gathering to talk about the killing. At the Rainbow Cafe, Woodrow Clardy sat tugging at his black mustache while he talked to Hendrix Rector and Carlos Hurd. Sometimes they were joined by Johnny Worthington.

"'Well, what're we gonna do about this thing?' said Hurd.

"'Yeah, we gonna let some black man kill a guy like Tom?' one of the drivers asked.

"Clardy pulled his mustache angrily and shook his head. Johnny Worthington didn't talk much but his eyes were hard and his jaw line tense. 'Fat' Joy came up.

"'Hey, are we going to let that guy cut up one of our pals, boys?'

"They were all mad but nobody was saying what to do. Then Worthington suddenly spoke up.

"'Hurd, you're from Pickens, ain't ya?'

"'Yep.'

"'You know the jailer?'

"'Sure, guy by the name of Ed Gilstrap, why?'

"''Cause I think we ought to go to see Ed tonight.'

"'Hey, now you're talking, Johnny.'

"'We need to go to that jail and get that s.o.b. tonight!'

"'That's right, Johnny. Let's go get him,' chimed in Rector, his face flushed with anger. Clardy and Hurd nodded in vehement agreement.

"'I was born and raised in Pickens. I can walk right in that jail,' said Hurd.

"'And then what, Johnny,' asked Woodrow Clardy.

"'Woody, you ain't never seen the likes of what's going to happen to that fellow!'"

*　*　*

"At two and a half hours after midnight a hot-tempered young man named Duran Keenan answered the phone in the Commercial Cab office. The caller asked, 'Are you ready to go with us?' Duran wanted to know what he meant and there was a short laugh at the other end of the line. A voice replied, 'Go over to Pickens and get that black guy who stabbed Brown.' The call was one of many made that night.

"When Keenan reached the Yellow cab office twenty or thirty men were elbow to elbow in the small room and a bottle of whiskey was making the rounds. Keenan cradled it with both hands tipping it up while the raw, liquid fire rolled down his throat. He drove by the home of a friend, awakened him and pretended to want to borrow a shotgun for rabbit hunting in Georgia. Taking the double-barreled shotgun and a box of shells, Duran Deenan headed for the river meeting place.

"At least six other cabs had already arrived. Woodrow Clardy was driving the lead car, and in the front seat with him were Carlos Hurd and Johnny Worthington. The procession of cabs began to stalk their prey following one another down the road from Easley to Pickens in the gloom and darkness of the February morning. They reached the outskirts of Pickens at about four-thirty.

"The jail was a grim old fortress. Within, all was dark. In the minutes before the men arrived, Jailer Ed Gilstrap slept peacefully. Of his two prisoners who shared the strange coincidence of the same last name, James Earle slept the deep sleep of a drunk. And, Willie Earle? Maybe he dreamed of his long bus ride from Virginia or of Sheriff W. H. Maulden arresting him the afternoon before.

"The procession of cabs was now within a block of the jail.

" 'Not a policeman in sight.' said Worthington chuckling. 'If they are they're too scared to come around!'

"Clardy and Hurd pounded on the door of the jail. In a few minutes they heard the key turn and the jailer opened the door.

" 'You know me, Gilstrap.' asked Hurd.

" 'Sure. What do you want this hour of the morning?'

" 'I want the man who killed Brown.'

" 'Carlos, you know I can't let you have him. You're going to get us all in a peck of. . . .' And then he saw Hurd's shotgun and just behind him Duran Keenan with his double-barreled, rabbit-hunting gun.

"'Wait'l I put some clothes on, Carlos,' said Gilstrap and went to his room. In a few minutes he was back and Paul Griggs, Clardy and Hurd followed him into the cell block.

"'There are two prisoners back there,' said Gilstrap. 'Which of them do you want?' Entering the cell block they stopped and looked in the first cell. The inmate looked at them and cringed. Then he began to whine, 'I'm not the one. He did it, not me!' The men looked at him, then motioned to the jailer to open the door to the next cell, Willie Earle's.

"Clardy and Hurd grabbed him and with Grigg's help they half carried the frightened man down the steps and pushed him into Clardy's car. Clardy, Hurd and Rector got in the front seat after shoving Willie Earle in the back between Worthington and Walter Crawford. The procession of cabs started back toward Easley.

"'I want to know why you killed Brown,' said Worthington.

"'I didn't kill him.'

"'The hell you didn't!'

"The cab behind them blew its horn and Clardy pulled over to the shoulder. They were near the Saluda dam. Men swarmed out of the cars. Ernest Stokes was the first to reach the cab.

"'He says he didn't kill him,' Crawford said.

"'Git out, Crawford! I used to be a deputy sheriff. I know how to get a confession out of a man.' He scrambled into the back seat. A man's scream came from the interior of the cab. 'He's owned it fellows,' said Stokes jumping out.

"Everyone loaded into the cabs again and the procession went on until it reached Bramlett Road. They were near the slaughter yards when Clardy stopped with the rest of the cars behind him. Stokes came up and opened the rear door. He pulled out his pocket knife.

"'Before you kill him, I want to put the same scars on him that he put on Brown.'

"'Get him outa my car, if you're gonna kill him,' hollered Clardy. Several of the men, all eager to get at Willie Earle, began trying to pull him out of the car. There was the sound of clothes ripping. The black man held on to the back seat but his fingers finally loosened and he was dragged bodily from the cab.

"A tall, slender boy with bushy hair struck the black in the mouth and knocked him down. Rector and Griggs hit him while Marvin Fleming beat him in the head with the stock of his shot gun. Some of the men tried to get in blows with sticks. And then Stokes dived in wielding his knife like a madman.

" 'Lord, you've killed me!' came a terrible cry from Willie Earle.

"Hurd shouted, 'Give me the gun. Let's get it over with!' He shot Willie Earle in the head and called out for more shells. The he shot him twice. Afterward everyone was more quiet. They got in their cabs and when they reached the still dark city of Greenville, the cabs fanned out—disappearing. Johnny Worthington was the only one that went right back to work. He picked up a few fares at the Railroad Station before he went off at eight o'clock.

"His daughter was just getting up when he came in.

" 'Well, we got rid of one,' he announced to her.

" 'Dad, what are you talking about?'

" 'I'm talking about the one that killed Brown,' he answered.

" 'My God, dad, you shouldn't have done it! What did you tell the dispatcher?'

" 'Dick Curton? Why, we told him before we left what we were going to do,' her father said angrily and went to bed."

*   *   *

Thirty-one men were charged with murder on February 21, 1947, and three months later on May 21st all the defendants tried were acquitted by a jury of their peers.

But it wasn't long before a strange story began to go around among the drivers, a story they really didn't want to talk about. Something eerie and horrible had been encountered late at night on Bramlett Road.

And in a small town not far from Greenville a waitress recently confided to a customer that her husband was one of the cab drivers who was there the night of the lynching.

"My husband's dead now," she said. "But I never saw anything like his face when he came home one night about a year before he died. He had been called out on Bramlett Road and something really frightened him. When he came home he was trembling so he could hardly talk.

"After awhile he turned to me and said, 'Mae, I saw that black man tonight,' and I said, 'Who do you mean?' But I knew for some things you just don't talk about are always there in the back of a person's mind.

"And then he turned and looked at me straight and said, 'I saw the ghost of Willie Earle. He's come back, Mae.'"

XIII

The Hound of Goshen

"... And what is death? ... Do you know it?" "Ey! I
know it," answered the old Negro woman. "... Hit's er
shadder en er darkness. ... En dat shadder en darkness
hit comes drappin' down on yer, creepin' up on yer; hit
gits hol 'er yo' feet. Den hit slips up ter yer knees, den hit
slips up, up twel hit gits ter yo' breas'. Dat reap-hook hit
gi's er wrench ter de breaf er you' mouf, en dar! Yer gone,
caze yer breaf, hit's yer soul!"

—Eli Shepard

The night around him was black as pitch and there were
ragged snatches of fog in the low places. It was late June of
1967 and Jim Garrett strode angrily along old Buncome Road
near Newberry, South Carolina. He was a tall, heavyset young
man who walked with a slightly rolling gait. There had been
another bitter quarrel with his father who had told him he
must stay and help on the family farm, one hundred and
sixty acres of red clay which would one day be his to till as
his father and grandfather had done before him.

For years he had dreamed of going to the university for he
hated farming. Three weeks ago he had graduated from high
school, and many of his classmates were making plans. But
he had only listened for he was afraid he would not be among
them. Tonight he was ready to explode with frustration. He
was on his way to talk with his friend and mentor, Paul Durell. What would he say? Was there any way he could work
and go to school without his father's help?

It was almost two miles to the Durell house from his own.
The banks were high on both sides of the road and it was

lined with woods. Even on moonlight nights this was a dark journey, but he had never minded it. Tonight the air was warm and humid and all about him were the night sounds of myriad cicadas and tree frogs squeaking and rasping as they practiced their invisible rituals.

He must have been a hundred feet beyond the cemetery when he sensed that something was following him. Stopping at the edge of the woods, Jim broke off the first sturdy branch he could find. Ever since childhood he had heard stories about this road but he was sure they were superstitions for he had walked the old Buncombe Road many a night.

In school, Jim was always the skeptic laughing at other boy's stories of ghosts or haunted places. He was convinced that science had an explanation for everything. In fact, it was his studies in science and mathematics that he was eager to pursue at the university. He brushed the old tales from his mind tonight as he might brush the cobwebs from a corner of his room.

Suddenly, a shadowy form seemed to dart from the woods and disappear into the underbrush on the opposite bank. The moon must have come out briefly and cast a beam of light across the road thought Jim. The Durell house was still a mile away and he found himself hastening his pace.

He had walked on a few feet when he was sure he felt something glide against the back of his legs and his forehead broke out in cold sweat. For the first time in years he vividly recalled the stories of this road, tales of a fearsome ghost dog that had staked out a five-mile stretch as its own!

But that was a hundred years ago and 1967 was a time of enlightenment. He could scarcely believe that a ghost dog had ever struck terror into the hearts of travelers down the onetime stagecoach route between Ebenezer Church in Maybinton Township and Goshen Hill in Union County.

He recalled his father telling him about the dog haunting this area near the columned Douglass mansion on the high bluff overlooking the road. Stripped down to the dark wood

The ghost dog staked out the Old Buncombe Road as his own. Reports of encounters with the hound of Goshen have been made as recently as the summer of 1982.

by many years of weathering, windows staring emptily with broken shutters askew, the house had always looked eerie as long as he could remember. It was up there somewhere on the bluff just ahead of him, and tonight he would be glad when he had passed it.

He knew that a Dr. Jim Coefield, once a much respected physician of the area, had seen the dog and was never able to explain it. Coefield's own dog which often accompanied him had left the road that night to scurry off through the woods and returned only after the apparition had vanished.

Then there was Berry Sanders' story. As a boy Sanders had worked for a Mr. Watt Henderson and every Saturday night he had to go through Goshen on his way home. One night in mid-April as he left the Oaks, he was closing the big iron gate when he heard a noise. Looking back Sanders saw a monstrous white dog, teeth bared, racing after him. To his horror, the dog passed right through the closed gate.

Berry's home was a mile away and he ran every foot of it. Once he turned his head and the huge animal was so close he could see its fiery eyes. It was a sight to curdle his blood and he was terrified but as he reached the safety of his home, the awesome creature turned and disappeared into the woods.

It was while Jim was recalling all this that he found he was no longer alone. There, bounding along behind him, was a dog larger than any he had ever seen. The animal was close upon him, ready to spring. His heart leaped within him. He spun around and with all his strength brought the stick down full across the animal's face but to his astonishment felt no resistance at all. The stick had passed right through the beast's head and the slavering, gaping mouth and enormous eyes like balls of fire were still hurtling through the air toward him.

Jim Garrett's feet took wings. He flew down the road and as he ran his chest began to ache. His breath came in tortured gasps but the dog remained right beside him. He was terrified. On he went, the dog staying abreast. Its eyes blazed, the tongue lolled between sharp white teeth, and the mouth appeared ready to devour him.

He was alone on the road and there was only the sound of his pounding feet. Soon, he became unaware of pain. His legs ran on as if independent of his body. He heard panting beside him, felt an icy pressure against his leg and then came a howl so unearthly it seemed to emanate from the very depths of hell.

Garrett had hunted with dogs and was not afraid of them but at this moment he knew *he* was the prey. He was being chased like the fox. He knew for the first time the paralyzing fear of the rabbit. The jaws of this monster would soon close about him and agonizingly kill him. Jim stumbled and fell. His last recollection was one of a tremendous weight upon his back.

When he awoke the morning sun shone warm on his face. He lay at the edge of the road beside the driveway to the old Douglass house. His collar felt wet and when he examined it he saw that it was stained with blood. There were marks on his shoulder near the throat and although the wounds were not deep, they resembled nothing so much as the marks of a dog's teeth.

As the man behind the counter of the store in Newberry tells this story, it has been almost fifteen years since his encounter with the apparition. But, it is obvious from the expression in his eyes that the horror of the experience remains.

A month later his father died. And the tall fellow with curly black hair says, "I will always believe that dog was an omen of death and even now I wouldn't care to walk that road alone at night."

XIV

There Goes Martin Baynard's Carriage!

Martin Baynard folded the fine white fabric into a tie, arranging it in a jaunty fashion about his neck. He tucked it neatly into his rich silk vest, his fingers giving it a final pat. It was just the right touch and he would cut quite a figure in his new suit. He was aware of this with a sort of comfortable confidence that was not really conceit.

Victoria could scarcely have found a handsomer bridegroom and as his thoughts turned to her his pulse beat more quickly. He, too, was lucky and he knew it. Even during the years spent abroad, he could not recall a girl that even compared with Victoria. Her black hair, long-lashed green eyes and creamy skin were all part of her great beauty. But it was more than that. There was an animation and excitement about her that he had sensed immediately. She was a creature of countless moods, and Martin loved her in every one of them.

They had met here on Hilton Head Island scarcely a year ago and it was surprising the meeting had not occurred sooner for their fathers were both well-to-do planters. Young men from surrounding plantations swarmed around Victoria and at first she did not appear to take his attentions seriously and barely acknowledged his presence. Not that Martin would not make a good match for his family was respected and wealthy, but the gossip of the chaperones behind their fans was that Martin had left some broken hearts in his wake.

Victoria had heard the whisperings and disapproving glances of which Martin himself was not even slightly aware. The Christmas season was full of balls, musicals, and oyster roasts on the beach, and almost the entire spring passed before Victoria even allowed him to see her without the entourage of suitors and friends that usually surrounded her. He was a tall, strikingly good-looking young man but seemed to be as serious-minded as herself. Victoria could certainly see nothing of the Don Juan about him.

Like his father, Martin had been educated in England. He was not given to gossip or small talk about their circle of friends. Nor did he appear to be interested in expounding on horses and hunting or rice or cotton. He liked to discuss serious issues and he knew many of the most important South Carolinians. Why he even knew George Washington!

On his part, he was delighted to discover such a quick mind behind the lovely face. Sometimes they would voice a thought at the same moment and glance at each other in happy surprise. By the time the yellow jessamine was festooning the trees, they were seeing each other almost daily. In mid-June, to the suprise of no one who had observed them together, John and Elizabeth Stoney announced the engagement of their only daughter, Victoria Ann.

From then on the pair would ride out each afternoon in Martin's cabriolet. Sometimes the graceful carriage would be seen speeding along the beach near the surf in the late afternoon. Victoria's bonnet would be off, her hair swept back from her face by the wind. The wedding was to take place in August, and at the Stoney plantation the most elaborate plans and preparations were taking place. In his happy and carefree state, Martin scarcely cared to be bothered with details and Victoria had never shown any great interest in the planning of social events.

When they did not ride along the beach there were leisurely drives down pleasant, winding, sandy roads. One afternoon they stopped to drink from a stream, tethering the horses to a tree at the edge of a patch of woods.

"Isn't that a graveyard over there among the trees," said Victoria.

"We can see," said Martin and hand in hand they walked

through dead leaves, skirted briars and soon were in the midst of some sandy depressions marked by headboards of wood with crudely carved letters. But most interesting to Victoria was a fresh grave which appeared to be that of a child. She reached down and picked up a small, primitive doll. There was also a plate and a cup. "Do you think the little thing drank out of this cup, Martin?"

"Probably."

"And, look. Here is a lamp. Why would they put that out here?"

"Perhaps, to light her way to eternity. It's strange they would believe she needed that, isn't it."

Victoria fondled the doll. "This is probably something she loved and played with. She must have liked this bright red dress."

"I wish you wouldn't touch those things, Victoria."

"Why? Do you think I am being disrespectful to the dead?"

"Of course not. I didn't mean that."

"Someone has treated this grave more rudely than I. Look at the pieces of broken pottery scattered over it." Even as they stood there looking around them, it had grown darker. Victoria stroked the hair on the head of the doll and there were tears in her eyes.

"I wonder how old she was and if she suffered much?"

"Victoria, for heaven sakes put that doll back on the grave and let's go!"

"I am. But you needn't speak to me like that. Are you afraid of ghosts in a cemetery?"

"No, I'm not afraid of ghosts but the Gullahs have different beliefs from ours and. . . ."

"And you believe their superstitions?"

"No, but there is a dark side to some of their beliefs, Victoria, and it is hard not to think about them sometimes. I have always heard that to appear too healthy or too happy provokes the evil spirits, and we are very happy."

"Oh, Martin! What sort of talk is that? The first thing we will do is find ourselves a smutty-nosed cat to bring us luck!

The Baynard family mausoleum was vandalized years ago.
Martin was buried here in the cemetery of Zion Chapel of Ease.

Does that satisfy you?" she said laughing up into his face. He looked at her adoringly. It was now less than a week until their wedding.

With more patience than usual, Victoria had endured the lengthy discussions and fittings for her wedding dress and other new gowns. This was a relief to Mrs. Stoney who placed great importance on that stream of endless minor decisions and duties which make up the warp and woof of daily life. Her greatest satisfaction was to immerse herself in a constant dither of activities, riding the crest of them and emerging with all seemingly overwhelming details conquered.

Some of the wedding guests would be coming from afar and must be lodged at the Baynard and Stoney plantations. Mrs. Stoney spent hours at her small Chippendale escritoire writing lists of preparations to be made. A whole sheep and a pig were to be roasted. Hams, turkeys, and chickens would be baked along with loaves of bread and biscuits without number. A barrel of sugar and one hundred dozen eggs would be needed for the cakes, jelly whip, and custard, not to mention citron pudding and coconut. Mauma, the black housekeeper's daughter, had been set to cutting paper to dress the stands for several long tables that would seat one hundred and fifty guests.

Finally, the day before the wedding arrived and in the warm August dusk, Victoria sat before the long gilt mirror in her bedroom. Her Gullah maid, Bina, brushed her thick, dark hair in long even strokes. Like many of her people, the girl's name was the word for Tuesday, the day she was born. Victoria knew that the *Wanderer* had brought in an illegal cargo of slaves a few weeks ago, but her father was so rigid in his conviction that the South Carolina economy rested upon the institution, she couldn't discuss it with him. He would become almost choleric with anger and leave the room if she so much as touched upon the subject.

As the girl brushed her hair she could hear her saying something under her breath over and over again.

"Bina, what are you saying?"

"Nothing, Missy, nothing."

But then she heard the words once more and they were "Hu hu. Dem pak, pak, pak." She understood for she had heard the Gullah language since she was a child. Bina was saying that she had heard an owl go knock, knock, knock against the window of the house in a vain attempt to get in.

This was a Gullah superstition, a bad omen, an omen of death, but Victoria only smiled and shook her head reprovingly. She could not get Bina to smile, however, for the girl's frightened eyes stared back at her from the mirror. Bina's practiced fingers arranged each strand of hair so that it framed her face prettily. Ready to go downstairs, Victoria impulsively grasped Bina's hand and drew her across the hall to show her the wedding finery her mother had arranged. There on the bed, awaiting the morrow's wedding, lay the spotless linen all crimped, the drawers with the fine tucks and lace insertion, the white silk stockings, the small white satin slippers and dress, the plain lace over the long bridal veil and wreath of white flowers, the short kid gloves with the deep lace frill. A diamond pin, a pair of gold earrings and a gold bracelet completed the attire. Bina gasped at all this spendor and stretching out one small, dark finger stroked the hem of the rich, satin gown.

As Victoria walked through the large downstairs hall she could hear the sound of laughter outside. Clinton and Harry, two young cousins from Columbia, had arrived and were being shown the cottage near the house where they would stay during the wedding festivities. Her brother Edmund's voice could be heard welcoming them.

For a moment, Victoria stood very quietly in the doorway to the parlor looking at her father's much loved face in repose. Captain John Stoney, a glass of Madeira wine on the table beside him, looked up from his book as Victoria entered the room.

"What are you reading?"

"The Planter's Bible, my dear."

"And by that, I presume you mean Montaigne. I find him most interesting."

"And, what do you know of Montaigne, young woman?"

"Oh, I have read some of his essays."

"And I suppose you have read what knowledge and occupation is best for a woman?" He patted her hand which rested on the arm of his chair.

"I believe Montaigne says it is the science of housekeeping, dear Papa, but sometimes I find so many things I enjoy doing more."

"Then you must consider his essay on not being willful, my dear. In our ignorance we often make judgments that are wrong."

Victoria picked up a copy of Shakespeare which lay at her father's elbow.

"Well, there are certainly some ladies not afraid to make judgments in here."

"My dear, a woman should be full of grace—modest and pliable."

"Like Momma?" Victoria's lovely lips curved in a delightful, teasing smile, but before her beleaguered Pappa could reply the sound of Martin's voice could be heard and the butler announced him.

"Come in, my dear fellow, come in," said Stoney rising. He was a tall, vigorous man even in his sixties. He had enjoyed sports during his years at Cambridge and this love of exercise combined with an excellent education and inquiring mind, suited him admirably for the amount of physical work and management involved in a plantation. John Stoney had a passing knowledge of many trades and this was good for everything was done on the plantation. The planter must know the right lay of his land and how it should be prepared. Much effort went into the training of unskilled laborers in a variety of tasks such as might be found in a small village for the plantation was sufficient unto itself. Captain Stoney occupied himself from early morning until the time his animals were stabled. After supper he often sat in the library and read as he was doing now.

The days of his wife Elizabeth were also busy. It was to her that the servants looked if they had problems or were sick. Elizabeth Stoney often read them chapters from the Bible, prayed with them, preached morality and sometimes had more influence than Stoney himself. As Victoria had sometimes heard the blacks say, "The plantation belongs to Master, but Ole Master belongs to Miss 'Lizabeth."

"Won't you and Mrs. Stoney ride with us?" offered Martin.

"Not this time, Martin. Mrs. Stoney is taking some medicine to the butler's wife who has been sick."

Martin helped Victoria into the barouche drawn by four beautiful blood bays. The carriage could be seen for awhile as it rolled down the moss-shrouded avenue of giant oaks until it disappeared in the growing darkness.

Outside the Baynard home slaves stood with flaming torches lighting the way of the arriving guests. Victoria dismounted beside a tabby step and Martin offered her his arm. Her dress was yellow silk and her dark hair rose above it like the dusky center of a magnificent golden daisy. Her cheeks were becomingly flushed and her eyes sparkled. The rug had been rolled back in the large ballroom and the floor waxed until its mirrorlike surface reflected the chandeliers like clusters of gleaming meteorites. Side tables placed along the walls of the immense room were laden with apples, oranges, almonds, raisins, butter mints and the finest sillabub. The mantles at each end of the ballroom were decorated with magnolia leaves and tall china jars filled with flowers.

Here and there clusters of guests chatted merrily and waited for the music to begin. The ladies were resplendent in fine muslin, India silk or satin, and for the most part, the men wore rich white silk vests and cravats.

Victoria was never lovelier and many a man watched enviously as Martin led her out on the floor to dance.

"I am of all men truly blest," Martin whispered into her ear.

"Why, I suppose we are both blest. Why must you look so serious my dear Martin?"

"It is my nature, I suppose, to believe that life for most people is something of a prison and death reaches them unfreed and still unblest."

"Martin, you have quite a morbid streak at times. They must escape their 'prison' as you call it."

At that moment the music stopped and Victoria's brother Edmund and his partner Betsy, a sweet-faced blonde who was on Hilton Head for the summer escaping from what the Charlestonian's called "the sickly season," turned to speak to them.

"Is your sister always so flushed after one dance or is it the excitement?" asked Betsy when the music had begun once again and they were a few steps away.

"No. She doesn't seem like herself," said Edmund watching her from a distance. But everyone, even Martin who noticed her high color and even greater vivacity than usual, thought it was excitement over the wedding to be.

The following morning he went out to the stable to be certain his carriage had been properly polished and decorated. Even in the shadows it gleamed and reflected his tall, straight figure. Martin was proud of his brougham built by Hooper for it was a most sought after vehicle. American carriage builders had borrowed the design from England where Lord Brougham had introduced it. Martin had left instructions that the elegant glossy, black carriage be decorated with white satin rosettes and ribbons. This morning his coachman stood waiting nearby impressive in his dark blue coat with silver braid, the Baynard livery.

Martin declined the coachman's gesture to assist him and they were on their way down the sandy, winding road that led to the Stoney plantation. As the white ribbons fluttered in the summer breeze Martin thought of the future. The months and years of happiness that lay ahead. There would be children and family holidays to celebrate—the warm, tender companionship of later years built on memories. All of this passed through his mind, not in detail, but with the vision the heart holds fast and gives up only with the deepest anguish.

It was a clear, bright morning and pine needles glistened in the summer sunlight. He was aware of the songs of birds, of the beauty all around him. It was one of those rare occasions when he felt a part of it all and joyously alive. After awhile these pleasant pictures gave way to a lightheartedness that Martin seldom felt for there was a certain melancholy spirit that had always existed in the core of his being. On either side of the carriage the marsh grass passed as if he rode through the midst of a silken green sea.

His happy trance was broken by the sudden awareness of a small black fleck on the horizon which began to move resolutely toward him. In a few minutes it was apparent that it was the figure of a horseman. Martin was puzzled. The rider was obviously riding at breakneck speed to become visible so soon.

Who could it be? No ordinary traveler would proceed at such a pace? In fact, it was no ordinary rider but one of the best horsemen he had ever known, his future brother-in-law Edmund. Victoria's brother reined in the animal and with a swirl of sand as the big bay's hooves wheeled about in the sand, he was beside the carriage. There was no smile on his face or in his gray eyes, only extreme distress.

"Martin, I have bad news for you. Victoria was extremely ill all night. A physician has been sent for and is at this moment on the way to her." Martin was so stunned he could scarcely believe he had heard Edmund rightly.

"Edmund, for God's sake, what is wrong with her?"

"I don't know, but there are symptoms of the country fever." Martin's face whitened, his jaw tensed and his blue eyes stared straight ahead as if he could not bear to look at Edmund. Tethering his horse to the brougham, Edmund got into the carriage with the silent Martin. Indeed, he scarcely spoke during the drive to the house. Edmund tried to relieve Martin's anxiety saying that even now the doctor was probably there and would hasten Victoria's recovery.

"I pray to God, he will," was Martin's terse response.

When they reached the Stoney plantation, a canopied, dusty phaeton was coming down the avenue of oaks toward them as they approached the house. A gray-haired, ruddy-faced man leaned out of it.

"She has an extremely high fever, gentlemen."

"May I see her, doctor?" asked Martin.

"I am sorry, my good fellow. You may not."

"But, Sir——"

"Martin, she is delirious. The answer is no."

Baynard reluctantly acquiesced. The doctor, after promising that he would return to see Victoria that evening, lightly swatted the rear of his large black and white pony and drove on.

Victoria's father stood waiting for them on the piazza. Worried as he was, he was the picture of composure and every inch an aristocrat. There was the striking white hair, olive skin, generous, finely chiseled mouth and expressive topaz eyes. Eyes that despite his calm, clearly showed deep anxiety. Mrs. Stoney came out of the depths of the house and joined her husband just as Edmund and Martin hurried up the piazza steps.

"Good morning, Martin. We are distressed at having such bad news for you. Papa, why don't you go in and rest awhile."

"How is she now, Mrs. Stoney?" asked Martin.

"About the same, Martin. She has been delirious most of the night."

Mr. Stoney excused himself "to rest for an hour" and his wife beckoned to Edmund and Martin to follow her into the parlor. They discussed guests to be notified at nearby plantations and Martin noticed several notes on the table in Elizabeth Stoney's handwriting, writing that was strong and bold for a woman. Even at such a moment he noticed that.

The notes were to be sent with others that he and Edmund had suggested and one of the servants was standing at the door now to see that they were dispatched.

They explained that Victoria was ill and the wedding could not take place at this time. Martin could scarcely believe it. He looked through the door of the parlor at the stairway. How often had he visualized his bride descending it in her "going away" clothes. There would be no wedding voyage tomorrow from Savannah to England. Martin arose and stepped out into the cool, semidarkness of the large hall finding a seat on the velvet-covered Chippendale sofa.

The fever would pass, he thought. Victoria would soon be as healthy as ever. Suddenly, he was aware that he was not alone. Someone was just a few feet away.

"Who is there?" he called but no one answered. A figure appeared almost at his elbow and he reached out roughly.

"Oh, Mr. Martin, don't hurt me!"

"Bina, it's you. I'm not going to hurt you. Why didn't you answer me."

"She goin', Mr. Martin. She goin'. I knew when I heard hu, hu, dem pak, pak, pak." There was a note of mystery and dark foreboding in the soft voice. He understood her meaning and became angry which only frightened Bina more.

"Don't you tell Miss Victoria that, Bina! Do you hear me?" She nodded miserably. "Is she awake?" Bina tried to reply but began crying and shaking her head. He took that to mean Victoria was still delirious. Releasing Bina he sank back on the sofa emotionally spent. He must have slept there until late afternoon. He got up and went upstairs seating himself in a chair in the hallway hoping that Mrs. Stoney or Bina would come out of Victoria's room and tell him something about her condition.

He had not sat there long before Mrs. Stoney rushed out of the room sobbing. He did not wait for permission to enter. There lay Victoria, her eyes closed and upon her face a waxy pallor. He pulled her to him but she did not open her eyes.

Hugging her against his breast he was suddenly struck by the stillness of the form in his arms. He gazed at his beloved closely. Victoria was dead.

Martin was startled to hear someone gasp and run from the room. Bina had been standing just behind him and he found her out in the hall.

"De God wok, Mr. Martin. De God wok," the girl said in Gullah.

"No Bina. It is not God's work. It is the work of the devil!" Martin left the Stoney home, his eyes wild and his expression tragic. Edmund tried to stop him at his carriage and calm him but all Baynard would say was, "The temptest strikes!" and off he rode, the carriage careening down the road.

Inside the coach Martin was filled with rage. He ripped off whatever ribbons his angry fingers could reach and shouted imprecations at God, bitter accusations punctuated by the sound of tearing satin, and all the while he cried great, gasping sobs.

The funeral was held the day after Victoria's death. Martin arrived at the Stoney plantation just before the carriages were to set out and the gleaming, black coach now arrayed with black satin rosettes and streamers took its place behind that of the family. The Stoney's were shocked at the appearance of his grief-ravaged face.

Yielding to Martin's impassioned pleas, the Stoney's had agreed to Victoria's body being interred in the Baynard mausoleum. The door gaped open and now they were gathered around it. Martin did not leave his coach. Mrs. Stoney, in a high-necked black silk dress with her hair drawn back severely, looked years older. At her right stood Edmund, pale and hollow-eyed. Behind them were some of the family slaves. Bina stood a little apart from the rest with her face expressionless and her brown eyes enigmatic. Perhaps, she was pondering 'de God wok' or wondering why Miss 'Lisabeth urged her to worship a god who would allow her young mistress to be taken on the eve of her wedding.

With her people, at night around the firesides there was

talk of powerful charms that could cure sickness and of the return of the spirits of the departed. Bina may have thought of this for she gave a slight, almost imperceptible shiver as she stared into the darkness of the mausoleum. One tightly closed hand grasped a small piece of broken pottery. Before she left she would find an opportunity to drop it beside the mausoleum.

Inside his coach, Martin sat alone. He could not believe his Victoria would actually be placed in one of the cold, stone crypts. His memories of her were so strong that even at this moment he could feel her presence as if she were right at his side. He watched Mrs. Stoney for she held a white rose which in a moment she would place on Victoria's casket.

Then, in the midst of the scripture reading there came an explosive, crash of thunder. "The tempest strikes!" thought Martin. The guests were stunned to see the Baynard coach, darkly magnificent in its funeral decor, dart from its place in line and hurtle out of the cemetery.

"What possessed Martin to behave so?" Edmund asked his father on the way home.

"What did you say his words were when he left the house yesterday after Victoria's death?"

"Something about a tempest striking him."

"Ah, I know."

"You know what?" said Edmund, more the huntsman than the scholar.

"Arnold's poem, *A Summer Night*, is what I think he meant. A man escapes the prison of life but before any blessing befalls him the tempest strikes him and between the lightning-bursts is seen only as a driving wreck!"

"Good Lord! That's what he looked like today, wasn't it, a wreck." Mr. Stoney stared off in the direction the coach had gone and shook his head. The clouds were dark and threatening and it seemed to be gathering up its fury.

In the late afternoon a torrential rain fell accompanied by wild bursts of thunder and lightning. The drops of water were only a light patter on the roof when an old black man appeared at the back door of the Stoney home asking to speak to Mr. Stoney. He had served the household for years but had become so crippled that he moved close to the beach where he lived fishing and crabbing.

"Mr. Stoney. I seen it." The man was trembling with excitement. "I seen Martin Baynard's carriage with those four black horses just gallopin' down the beach. Right in the middle of that storm, and lightnin' was playin' all around that coach!"

Nor was the fisherman the only one for many saw the black coach being driven at breakneck speed along the beach, black satin streamers still dangling from it.

A week after the funeral a servant arrived at the Stoney's astride Martin's fastest horse, a two-year-old thoroughbred named Lafayette. Baynard had sent him with a message that he, like Victoria, had the dreaded fever and would die "with her name on my lips." And die Martin Baynard did, a week to the day after Victoria's funeral. He was interred in the Baynard mausoleum and at his request no service was held.

But strangely enough, the appearances of the carriage continued. On the very night Martin was taken to the cemetery there were reports of the rhythmic thunder of horses' hooves and the clatter of a coach rushing past. This happened through the years and some born with a caul and others, unaware of any special powers, have seen the carriage hurtling down the island roads in the moonlight or racing beside the foaming surf. There were always allusions to the black satin ribbons streaming in the wind.

Even today there are some who claim to have seen a vehicle coming toward them on stormy nights and between the flashes of lightning have been sure it was an old-fashioned coach passing them. Over a century has gone by but the story of the phantom coach lingers on at Hilton Head Island. If the pounding hoof beats should be heard late at night by a guest in one of the fine hotels, Martin Baynard's gleaming coach may be dashing by.

There are islanders who know the sounds full well and draw their curtains aside ever so slightly to watch this grieved and angry spirit passing in the night.

And when will Martin Baynard cease to drive his eerie funeral carriage? The older Gullah's say, "Not 'til Gabriel blow 'e horn."

XV

The Singing Portrait

The horse chose his footing carefully for the road was deep cut and the high banks added to the darkness. Joseph Newton was on his way home from his father's store. Fog lay like a white shroud in the low places of the old stagecoach trace. Joseph felt his horse tremble. The bay mare was a sensitive animal and he wondered what she had heard.

In a few minutes they were directly opposite the Douglass home. From the hill above, wafted on the early spring breeze, came a strange and beautiful melody. Newton had heard that the Douglass family was visiting friends in nearby Newberry. Even if they were not, what earthly reason could there be for music coming from the house at this hour?

Reining in the mare at the road leading to the house, Joseph decided to investigate. Sometimes, he had seen lights burning long after midnight in the doctor's little office building, but tonight both office and house were in darkness. The melody he had heard on the road was louder than ever. He mounted the porch, drawn despite himself.

Although, the tones had a certain weird quality, they were also enticing. The scent of yellow jessamine from the yard enveloped him as he stared in through the parlor window. The room was drenched in moonlight. He could see the fireplace and the chairs on each side of it and then he noticed the portrait. It had hung over the mantle for as long as he could remember, but it had never looked like this! The face of the beautiful woman stared at him. It was almost incandescent and the very canvas seemed to pulsate with life.

To his suprise he realized that the music was coming from

the painting. Newton was so petrified he couldn't move. The beautiful song seemed to hold him captive, surround him, possess him. He was unaware of how long he stood there listening. There was a shattering crash of thunder, and he was jolted out of his trance.

The music from the parlor ceased and the face in the portrait flickered like a candle flame and went out. Now the room was in total darkness. Staccato spatters of rain took aim at the house and at him. Wind hastened through the bushes and shook the bare branches of the tree tops sending down a shower of twigs. Then it was bright as day all around him and a sharp, explosive crack as if lightning had struck just a few feet away! Newton fled.

With fumbling fingers he untied the mare's reins from the hemlock, leaped on her back and as the rain swept down in sheets, horse and rider galloped away from the rambling old house. Like a pair of frightened phantoms they sped through the night and past the church yard, the white marble tombstones illuminated by flashes of lightning. Newton glanced toward the cemetery. He knew that "Miss Anna" was long dead and he also knew that it was her portrait that had always hung over the mantle. He was frightened and bewildered.

Anna Dixon Hardy had died on April 18, 1861. He recalled the big family picnics on the church grounds after service and the old lady everyone called "Miss Anna." Even though he had been a child, he could see her now, lips pressed sternly together; a steely glint in her gray eyes. And then the memories began to blur. How could the lovely face in the portrait be Miss Anna? All he knew was that he must see that face again.

The following night there was a full moon and Newton was determined to go back. Again fog from the river lay upon much of the road. He would mount a slight rise and come out of it and then he was part of that misty world again. Strange shapes would loom ahead of him, dark limbs reach out like twisted arms. He began to think this was a foolish errand and was only jarred from his reverie by the be-

Despite his fear he decided to enter the old house. The front door was unlocked. Then came a wild and eerie shriek!

havior of his mare. She would shy seemingly at nothing, walk ever more slowly until finally she came to a complete halt in front of the graveyard. Good Lord! Why did the animal have to stop here?

He prodded her sides sharply, and surprised by this unaccustomed treatment, the mare leaped ahead and was off running. He finally managed to slow her to a walk and held out his lantern to watch for the red clay ruts that would signal the driveway of the Douglass house. He began to think they had passed it when suddenly there was the road.

No wheel prints or hoof marks had been made that day in the damp earth, and the rain of the night before had obliterated the prints of his own horse. Everything was just as he had left it. No one had been in or out of the house.

Newton tethered his horse beside the porch. There was a rush of air past his face and he flung up his arm. Bats! Ugh, how he despised them. As he started toward the porch a cloud obscured the moon and for a few minutes all was blackness. Aware of the beating of his own heart and of every night sound, he felt his way up the steps to the window where he had stood the night before.

As if a hand had drawn aside a curtain, the cloud passed and moonlight streamed into the room. There was no music and the face of the portrait was scarcely visible. The moonlight was not upon it, but he felt certain the silvery streak on the wall would soon reach the portrait. He settled himself in a more comfortable position and waited.

He had not been there long when he heard a faint sound far off in the distance that he supposed to be the sound of a bird. But it was not the song of a bird at all. It was rather the soft, beckoning notes of a woman's voice raised in song. He gazed at the portrait. It was washed in moonlight. The music grew louder and a light appeared to emanate from the picture itself. He felt that he was looking far back into the portrait, much as one would gaze down a long corridor, and the face at the end of it grew more distinct as the music increased in intensity. The exquisite features and large, beautiful eyes assumed a startlingly alive appearance.

He had a sensation of being irresistibly drawn toward the picture and he decided to enter the house. He found the front door unlocked, the door to the parlor open, and the room flooded with light. The light had a bluish cast to it and he saw immediately that the picture was its source. He stood and listened as the alluring voice sang on and on.

But he could not see the eyes and he knew he must look the woman full in the face. He stepped into the path of light but he had no sooner done so than he heard a wild and eerie shriek. He shuddered but continued to look at the woman and as he did a change began to come over the portrait. The face was aging rapidly and in a matter of seconds there was Miss Anna. The white ruff was around her face in the severe style worn by elderly women of the Civil War era. Her lips were tightly compressed and the gray eyes, if anything, were hostile.

Fear shot through him like the blade of a knife. Outside his mare gave a whinney and Newton was ready to leave. He never returned and he always wondered about the portrait. Others heard the nocturnal music but few stayed long to investigate.

No one lived in the old house after the 1950s and it was devoid of furnishings but the "Singing Portrait" still exists. It was discovered in the home of Miss Anna's great-granddaughter, Mrs. J. T. Ritchie, near Greenwood, South Carolina.

"As yet, I haven't heard it sing," said Mrs. Ritchie.

"But I do remember from my youth how her eyes never seemed to leave me when I practiced the piano there in the parlor. Even now I can recall the feeling that they were watching me."

The painting itself is an artistic treasure for it was done by the internationally-known artist, John Scarborough. During the first half of the nineteenth century, Scarborough painted many prominent people as well as Miss Anna. How could he have known that one of his portraits would be used to help the ghost of a once beautiful woman return?

XVI

The Spirit with the Tradd Street Address

"I wish I had kept a journal of the strange things that have happened over the last ten years in this house."

It was a raw winter day in Charleston and we sat watching the flames in the Adams fireplace with our toes near the brass fender. I was surrounded by eighteenth-century furniture and handsome gilt mirrors. My hostess and I sipped sherry from a Waterford decanter as she continued her story.

"I can't say I've ever seen it close enough to describe the face, but I'm sure we have a ghost living here with us. For years I would never have believed it and even now I don't go around telling people. There would probably be strangers peering in the windows of the house and we would have to start locking the garden gate. I should hate to do that."

Her well-manicured hands were raised in a gesture of horror and the blue eyes sought mine for assurance that I understood and would respect her need for privacy.

"Sometimes, I have had friends here and noticed them looking around while they tried not to let me see them. That was when we could all hear the sound of footsteps but no one there. I know it was a ghost walking around and I know they heard it, too. They simply didn't know what to say.

"We would be sitting in my kitchen talking over a cup of tea when doors would open and close upstairs, and footsteps could be heard walking down the hall or in one of the bedrooms overhead. Sometimes a table would be knocked over and that was clearly discernible for there would be a loud crash to the floor. I would try to think of something amusing

Here on picturesque Tradd Street there is a house where a ghost lives.

to say to distract my guest from the sounds upstairs and gradually their startled expression would fade.

"Perhaps, because I ignored it they hesitated to say anything or they may have thought I had a private friend upstairs whose presence I didn't wish to acknowledge, although such a situation would be ridiculous in our neighborhood where we all know each other so well. Everyone's comings and goings are observed and even the hours we call the cat are common ken.

"One day my neighbor and I were here in the parlor having coffee when we heard the front door open. We waited expecting to hear a member of the family greet us, but all was quiet. There was a slight pause before we heard the door close and then we saw a shadow in the shape of a person pass across the wall of the hallway.

"Strange to say, my first thought was that we were using

my favorite Limoge cups and I wondered if my neighbor would drop one of them to the floor. I looked over at her and her hand was shaking badly so I said, 'Loretta, why not put your cup on the table and let me heat up your coffee just a bit?' She turned and gave me the strangest look but at least she put my cup with the gold band on the table. When I glanced back toward the hall I was distressed to see the shadow was still there and I hoped Loretta was busy with the sugar and cream.

"At that moment she grasped my arm and startled me nearly to death.

"'Marie, what in the world is out in the hall? You aren't fooling me a bit. Who is it?'

"All I could do was shake my head. What was there to say? I had no more idea than she. A moment later there was the sound of a footstep on the first tread, a pause as if someone were staring into the parlor, and then, very slowly, the footsteps went on up the stairs. We both sat there in absolute silence listening and after that, of course, there was nothing to do but tell her the things that went on in this house. Loretta was the only person other than my husband that I ever discussed these things with. We had been friends since college and I knew she wouldn't think I was crazy. Besides she had seen and heard it for herself.

"I suppose our visitors would gradually have been frightened away if this sort of thing occurred often but the ghost usually stayed upstairs except for those rare occasions when it left the house. I still wonder where it went, don't you? But how does one trail a ghost? As the first months in the house wore on, I became used to these comings and goings. Sometimes the hall light would go on or off about the time the front door would close.

"Incidentally, I am sure it is a woman. One night I had drawn the drapes and was getting ready for bed when I realized she had entered the bedroom. At first I stood there perfectly still not knowing whether to pull my slip over my head or not. I would never have done that if it had been a man. Then I decided there was nothing to do but undress and get into bed. By this time I had the strongest feeling it was a woman and that she meant no harm."

The story of the lady who lives in the house on Tradd Street will be resumed shortly. An interesting sidelight is the recollection of a nearby neighbor. Soon after her family moved to this street, the house which now belongs to her friend was occupied briefly during World War I by a very lovely young lady. She lived there with an older woman presumed to be her mother although little was known about the pair for they made no close friends in the neighborhood.

Possessed of that beautiful hair sometimes called Titian gold and creamy skin with a delicate apricot blush in her cheeks, the young woman created quite a stir among the men. They would call upon her and she entertained them in the parlor, the notes of her piano floating out in the darkness many an evening. Some said her voice was like that of a nightingale, but compliments were more effusive then.

At first, Térèse, as she was called, seemed to have no favorites but later it was whispered that just after midnight a limousine would park out in front of the wrought iron gate that opens on the garden at the side of the house. Before dawn it was always gone.

The only excursions Térèse made outside the house were for an occasional ride along the waterfront or to post a letter. This made her even more mysterious and some of the Charleston ladies would stop her on the street on some pretext such as asking the time of day and then attempt to strike up a conversation. The answers they received were invariably polite but brief.

Finally, one day Térèse confided to a neighbor that her mother was quite ill, and she was on her way to the pharmacy for a prescription. A few weeks later Térèse appeared on the street in an elegant black suit. There were dark smudges beneath her lovely eyes and her face was pale. She looked the picture of grief. There were some expressions of sympathy but considerable talk. Two of the ladies of the neighborhood, more curious than kind, called upon her to

Who knows behind which shuttered window the ghost appears?

express their condolences but she met them at the door and pleaded illness.

One morning the curtains were gone from the windows and the house was empty. A tradesman was heard knocking on the door but no one came. The neighbor who lived next to the garden said she had been unable to sleep the night before and had heard the motor of a car cut off and stop at the curb outside. When she went to the window and looked out she claimed to have seen the black limousine and a chauffeur holding the door open for a veiled woman.

Some months later Charlestonians who attend balls in Washington saw a beautiful Titian haired young woman on the arm of the German ambassador. They were convinced that the lady was the mysterious Térèse. And, if so what happened to the woman supposedly her mother? Was the elderly lady merely playing the role? And was it a masquerade that led to her death?

We can only speculate about what happened to the elderly lady and the identity of the ghost in the house on Tradd Street. But we do know that even the grown children of our friend who lives there today will not stay overnight in the house unless their mother is at home.

"One of my daughters, Carol who lives in Columbia, saw an elderly lady in a long white gown leaning over her in the middle of the night. She heard a woman's voice but could not understand the words. Then Carol's nightstand tipped over and crashed on the floor. Terrified she jumped from her bed and ran out of the room. I don't know how often she saw the woman. Carol always seemed more sensitive about the ghost than the rest of us. But when they come to Charleston, unless my husband or I am here, none of them will use this house."

The cheerful fire has died and left only a bed of glowing embers. The early dusk of a winter's day can be seen between the curtains. At any moment the front door in the hall may open quietly and the shadow of a woman begin to move across the wall.

XVII

The Ghost of Daufuskie Island

Daufuskie, the very name is filled with mystery. Owners of the colorful luxury boats that form a bright necklace around Hilton Head Harbor show little interest in the dark island across the water. Its dim, inscrutable shape just a few miles away is a different world, a world that resembles the beclouded past seen by early adventurers.

Twelve-year-old Nick Beatty loved the island from the day he and his family moved here. The shadowy gloom of the pine barrens became his domain; the sound of the ocean and calls of the sea birds, his music. Except for occasional trips with his family and days in the island's two-room school, Nick's life was not unlike that of a boy who might have lived on a South Carolina coastal island a hundred years ago.

When Nick, Jessica and Rusty were not marveling at strange sea creatures cast up on the beach or exploring the dense forest of live oaks, pines and cedars, there was another place that drew them like a magnet! It was the eerie old cemetery where stained stones, some crazily askew, marked the early graves. For the wealthier, there were elaborate, above ground mausoleums. But the children were most interested in one mausoleum which had a few bricks missing from the front. They left a black, gaping hole that attracted Nick's curiosity.

By placing his face against the cool brick and staring down into the darkness of the tomb below, Nick could see the coffins. One of them was curved like the body of a woman and it stood leaning against the back wall of the underground tomb. Who could she have been and why was her coffin left resting against the wall?

At Nick's new island home something was always happening. His father had begun to remodel the old house immediately. Trips were made to the mainland in the boat to bring back antique furnishings. When the weather was sunny and warm there were frequent picnics on the beach with his tall, graceful mother who had adapted happily to the island lifestyle.

While his parents were absent on trips to the mainland, there was always, Sal, a family friend, who stayed with Nick and his brother and sister. Sal, a friendly, fascinating man, was visiting from his native Italy. Soon he would return to occupy an inherited family castle. Sal was cheerful, good-natured and could usually be counted upon for a game of catch or Frisbee throwing, but one day they could do neither for it was raw and cold.

Nick helped Sal build a fire and while Sal sat reading his Italian language newspaper, Nick played solitaire on the floor. At first he was only faintly aware of something moving nearby. It must have continued for some time and been observed out of the corner of his eye, but what the mind cannot accept as possible, the eye often refuses to see. It may even have gone on for as long as half an hour before Nick admitted it to himself. When he did he just sat there staring, his hand with the card ready to play still in mid-air.

The rocker between him and Sal was rocking gently and noiselessly back and forth. Sal, absorbed in his newspaper, was oblivious to the motion of the chair almost beside him. At that moment there was the sound of footsteps on the porch and Nick looked toward the door. Christmas was just two weeks away and his mother and father were back from the mainland loaded with packages.

It was after the holidays before Nick saw anything unusual again. He and Sal were once more alone in the living room. Jessica and Rusty were off with their parents but Nick had wanted to say on the island with Sal.

Sal sat in his favorite chair. His head with the curly but graying hair had fallen forward on his chest, the deep set

This was the old Daufuskie lighthouse. The light was once perched on top of this gable. The Beatty family bought and remodeled the house.

Was Nick's friend actually the ghost of this old man? He was almost ninety when he died and had managed to hang on to his island home a longer time than most others.

eyes with their almost transparent lids had closed and he had dropped off to sleep. Nick could hear his measured breathing, each breath followed by a faint whistling sound at the end. It didn't disturb Nick's reading at all for he was used to it. But he was soon aware of a noise that was unfamiliar.

Upstairs the bedroom door closed and footsteps could be heard in the hall overhead approaching the stairs. Then, every so slowly, as though someone might be holding on to the rail, the footsteps could be heard again starting down the stairs.

Nick leaned over and shook Sal, holding a finger warningly before his own lips.

"Sal, wake up, wake up!"

"Wake up . . . why? Stop shaking me!"

"Be quiet! Can't you hear the footsteps?"

"Footsteps where?" But at least Sal was whispering.

"Coming down the steps."

"Into the room here where we are?"

"Yes."

Suddenly, Sal was alert as a cat listening for a sound in the night. The footsteps stopped.

Neither Sal nor Nick moved and for a time all was quiet. They heard the loud tick of the pine grandfather clock. They heard the beating of their own hearts. Then the footsteps started. This time they sounded as if they were beginning at the landing.

Nick gripped Sal's hand hard, not so much from fear as excitement. He knew how many steps there were and he began to count them. Four more to go, then three, then two and now the last step. Whatever it was must be here in the room with them. Nick and Sal stared over at the foot of the steps but no one was there.

"I heard someone coming down the steps, Sal. I know I did!"

Sal looked bewildered and uneasy but he tried to shrug it off.

"Yes, I heard something, Nick, but nothing is there."

"But you heard the noise, too!"

"All old houses have noises and this one is just like all the others."

"Noises, yes, but . . . Sal, look at that chair!"

A few feet from Sal was an old gooseneck rocker. Not the prettiest chair in the room for the flowered black damask was worn and even threadbare in places. But the chair itself was comfortable.

As Sal and Nick stared at it the chair rocked slowly back and forth and back and forth. Sal rose as if he would seize it, but the instant he started toward it the rocker stopped. Not gradually, nor slowly but as if an invisible hand had come down firmly on the arm of the chair and stopped it abruptly. Even then Sal never wanted to admit he had seen anything out of the ordinary.

A few weeks later Nick began to tell his mother stories of old shipwrecks that had happened near the island and of a terrible Indian massacre at the north end of Daufuskie. The settlers had endured many Indian attacks and finally, early one morning they came out to the island and fell upon the Indians.

"Mother, the water ran red with blood."

"Nick, where are you getting these stories?"

"From my friend, Arthur."

"Who is Arthur? Someone at school?"

"Of course not. Arthur is the old man with the white hair and the beard."

"I don't know any Arthur," said his mother with some irritation. "Nick, when and where do you visit this old man and talk with him?"

"I don't visit him, mother. He comes here to see me. Haven't you ever seen him sitting in the living room? He usually sits in the chair with the gooseneck arms."

His mother shook her head in amazement.

"I don't know why not. He often sits there rocking back and forth and some days we talk and talk."

Nick's stories about the island continued through the early spring but it was not until one day when his mother was asking one of the islanders about the history of the house that she began to guess who Nick's "friend" really was.

Just to be sure she decided to go by the cemetery on her way home. It didn't take her long to find the stone she was looking for. There it was, a simple, gray granite marker not as old as many of the others. On it was engraved the name Arthur Burns. Could a dead man be the source of Nick's stories?

Burns had been keeper of the Daufuskie light for many years and the home the Beatty family was living in had been the old lighthouse. Sometime, after his retirement and before his death, Arthur Burns had become quite ill and he was taken from the island to a hospital on the mainland. When he returned, it was said, that he had vowed no one would ever get him to leave his house again. The words he had used were, "I'm going to stay in this house forever!"

But all that really mattered to Nick was that he had a friend, a friend named Arthur who could tell the most fascinating stories a boy had ever heard.

XVIII

The Phantom Horseman of Columbia

Not far from the State House in Columbia, a lone figure with a Malacca cane in his hand made his way down Lady Street. Perhaps, the dampness in the night air was causing the old wound in Raymond MacDonald's leg to twitch with pain as it did tonight but despite this, he was still a strong and active man.

His large, black collie trotted along beside him as always and there was no premonition that anything unusual was about to occur in his life. He had left his daughter Elizabeth's house after a visit just as he had done so many other evenings and was strolling to his own home near the corner of Bull and Blanding streets. The fragrance of honeysuckle enveloped him. The streets were deserted and most of the large homes darkened.

Often, there was a light in the upstairs bedroom of the Frazier house. Yes, it was there tonight and he knew that Mrs. Frazier, a lovely woman who was widowed like himself, was probably reading.

At that moment his collie barked and he could feel the dog's body pressed against his leg almost throwing him off balance. What in the name of heaven was the matter with the animal! He cursed under his breath. Suppose Rex's barking disturbed the widow, and she thought that someone was lurking in the dense shrubbery surrounding the house.

"Hush, hush, Rex," he admonished and on he went for about fifty feet when the dog cowered and began to bark once more. He had never known Rex to behave this way for the dog was almost too brash and adventurous. He spoke to him comfortingly, patted him, and the animal's trembling subsided.

At that moment something large and white hurtled toward him out of the darkness. He had no time to even raise an arm to protect himself. There was the sound of whirring wings within inches of his face. It was an enormous white owl and its wing spread seemed to have been six feet. Then it was gone. MacDonald had stumbled, almost fallen, and recovered himself. The near collision with the owl had left him shaken.

He told himself that he was only feeling the tensions everyone was experiencing this spring of 1914 for there were ominous signs of war in Europe. Early that evening he had stood in front of a bulletin board with a crowd reading news of the German Kaiser's latest threats. Over that tinderbox of the Balkan's where wars were ignited, the German leader waved his saber and inflamed emotions while the world held its breath.

The corner of Bull and Blanding streets was only a short distance when the dog began to bark again. Seized with irritation MacDonald stopped to break a switch from a bush to chastise the animal. Could the full moon be disturbing the dog? His eyes searched the sky and as he looked toward the corner he saw a most astonishing sight.

High in the tops of the mammoth oaks was a sharply etched, ghostly figure of a horseman. He could see it plainly, shining silvery white against the leaves. It was like an equestrian statue; the horse and rider were of heroic size. He was able to pick out every detail. There was the saddle, the reins, the bridle—even the flowing tail. All were clearly defined. Amazed, he stood staring at the treetops and as he did, the horse reared up as if eager to be off on some far away mission.

As he watched he gradually became aware that he was not alone. A man and woman were walking on the opposite side of the street arm in arm. He watched curiously. The couple must have taken a room at the nearby lodging house for they were not from his neighborhood. They reached the opposite

MacDonald was not the only one who believed that the phantom rider was Wade Hampton.

corner completely unaware that he was standing in the shadows just across the street from them.

Suddenly, he saw the man raise his arm and point toward the tree tops. His companion looked upward and stifled a scream. "Hush, for heaven's sake!," he heard the man say and for a moment the pair stared at the sky. Then the woman broke free and began to run in the direction of the rooming house with the man close at her heels.

He knew the pair had seen the horseman as he had, and in a sense, he was reassured. There was no rational explanation for what he had witnessed and if it had not been for the obvious fright of the couple, he would have doubted his own senses.

Relieved, he reached his front door and after hanging his clothes in the wardrobe he lay down to sleep. But all night long he tossed and turned and refought the battles of years ago. Once more he was part of General Hampton's cavalry fighting from the Wilderness to Cold Harbor, sleeping upon the ground, thrusting his sword into wildly shouting men in blue, dimly aware of gray clad figures lying on the ground, hearing the frantic whinney of riderless horses panic stricken from the smoke and fire of battle.

The next morning he awoke to rays of sunlight coming through the tall windows of his bedroom, and knowing that it had been the sort of nightmare he had not suffered in decades, he fell back into an exhausted, dreamless slumber.

That evening after the cook left, he followed his usual custom of walking over to his daughter's home. When he arrived he saw immediately that she was bursting with excitement.

"Father, have you heard the news? Everyone is talking about a ghost horseman they have seen in the tree tops at the corner of Blanding and Bull streets. We want to see it. Will you walk over with John and me?"

Arriving at the site of the apparition, they found a crowd already gathered. Ten minutes passed, fifteen, a half hour and still there was nothing to be seen. Suddenly, there was the figure of the white horseman in the sky and a gasp rose from the crowd.

"It's one of the Four Horsemen of the Apocalypse," shouted an old man. "Oh, something evil is to come upon us that will ravage and lay waste this land!"

"Lordy, lordy," came a chorus of awestruck voices and above it could be heard a Negro woman crying out, "The angel Gabriel is fixin' to blow his horn. Our sins done foun' us out!" Again came the chorus of voices, "Oh, do Lord help us!"

Raymond told his daughter he had seen it the night before but could offer no explanation. Finally, a bank of clouds covered the moon and the horseman could no longer be seen.

Returning to his home he somehow felt impelled to go to the bottom drawer of the old mahogany wardrobe in his room and withdraw a pile of old pictures. One by one he sorted through them not really knowing why. It was almost midnight when his eyes fell upon the most treasured picture of the collection. It was the one of General Wade Hampton seated on his horse. He dropped the picture, and Rex who had been asleep on the floor beside him scrambled to his feet, began to howl mournfully, and with his tail between his legs ran from the room.

Raymond held the picture under the light and stared at the broadly built man under whom he had served in the Civil War. There were the great muscles of arm and leg, the wide square shoulders and strong neck with the large head carried high. The profile with the long side-whiskers was one of leonine handsomeness. It was a man he would have recognized anywhere, a man whose heroic figure had continued to inspire awe even during the last days of his life. But most important of all, it was the image in every detail of the phantom rider he had seen in the treetops.

When he awoke the following morning he was still in his chair, a glass of cognac he had poured was untouched on the table beside him and the picture had slipped from his hand.

Each night that spring crowds continued to gather to see the horseman in the sky and as time went on, MacDonald was not the only one who believed that the phantom rider was Wade Hampton. Had General Hampton returned to warn of turbulent days ahead? Was this a prophetic appearance before a time of crisis for the country?

Mrs. Jennie Clarkson Dreher of Columbia recalls having had the figure pointed out to her when she was a child, and it is a well-established fact that many saw it.

Appendix

Notes and Commentaries on the Stories

I.   The Ghost Hand

An interesting parallel exists to this story in accounts of the "black ghost" which terrified a family in an old Victorian home. The hauntings occurred in the Camp Road district of Leeds, England in 1932.

Knocks were followed by shuffling sounds upon the stairs and then the apparition appeared. Mrs. Annie Halliday, the owner of the house, first saw it early one morning. It was a huge man about six feet tall, dressed in a long black coat. He did not speak and Mrs. Halliday was shocked as she stepped toward him to question him to see him suddenly vanish.

It is also eerie to discover that a child in this house told her mother she had seen a tall man whom she first thought was her father, come toward her with fingers outstretched. This account is similar to Mrs. Royal's experience when she opened her eyes to find the man in the black coat standing over her with his hand reaching toward her.

Police records in Leeds were checked to see if there had ever been any tragedy in the house but nothing could be found. Mrs. Royal's mother seeing the ghost in the daytime demonstrates that apparitions are not just seen at night. Also, that the shades of the dead, or whatever we may call them, are by no means restricted to their burial place.

The very fact that the appearances of this ghost are occurring right now in a home in Summerville, South Carolina, makes us wonder if events like this are not happening in more homes than we might have realized.

II. The Mysterious Land's End Light

Hundreds of people claim to have seen the Land's End light near Beaufort. Sometimes it appears as a reddish glow, swinging over the highway and at other times it is seen as mercury blue, the color of a type of swamp gas that floats eerily through the wooded areas of the island.

The light on St. Helena's Island is not the only ghost light reported in South Carolina but it is certainly the state's most famous. North Carolina's best known places to view lights of the sort are Maco Station near Wilmington and the Brown Mountain lights near Linville. Both have been a magnet for scientific expeditions as well as the curious. Ghost lights are to be seen in many states and are not a rarity, only sound explanations of them. Scientists have come and gone but few conclusions have been reached.

Of course, there is such a thing as swamp gas. But there are many swamps with similar natural conditions and yet they have no reputation for ghost lights. Surely the same conditions on St. Helena's Island are duplicated in other parts of the coastal Carolinas.

The well-known light between Marfa and Alpine, Texas, has been seen since the days of the Indians and the earliest settlers. Although, the light appears each night and pilots from a nearby base have flour bombed it to attempt to mark its origin, the source has never been found. The country in this area is dry and mountainous and the possibility of swamp gas is most unlikely.

Folklore sometimes explains these lights as the spirits of Indian maidens searching for a lover killed in battle or the ghosts of men who died by decapitation returning with a lantern to look for their heads—and then there are stories that these lights are the spirits of the dead.

One of the most prevalent beliefs, and one that seemingly crosses barriers of race and degrees of civilization, is that ghost lights and ghosts are often linked to buried treasure. Some of the people who live along Land's End Road believe that residents of the area buried their family treasures during the Civil War and the light began at that time. But there is no generally agreed upon origin.

Only, that the light is there. It is unpredictable in its appearance and it is startling to behold.

III. The Haunted Castle at Beaufort

South Carolina ghostlore, as well as its history, has been influenced by the Spanish, French, and English. In Europe, during the Middle Ages, dwarfs were often employed as jesters by kings and prominent men. It was the duty of a jester to amuse, and like our modern-day clowns, they helped people forget their troubles. The jester was almost a member of the family taking part in their gatherings, sharing family secrets, and playing with the children. We understand the sadness of Shakespeare's Hamlet when he saw the skull of his father's jester, Yorick, unearthed by gravediggers.

Although, the jesters' capers produced laughter, they were also regarded with an attitude blending respect and caution that stemmed from Norse mythology. Dwarfs, sometimes called Nibelungs, were thought to possess special powers. According to Germanic folklore they knew the location of a golden treasure that cursed anyone who seized it.

Ancient legendry also refers to dwarfs as *children of the mist*. Can it be more than coincidence that this story of a dwarf is connected with a house so often surrounded by mist?

IV. The Hitchhiker of Highway 107

The ghost hitchhiker of Highway 107 is not the only roadside specter in South Carolina for there is the Swamp Girl who has been reportedly picked up many times on her way to Columbia. And, in North Carolina lovely Lydia waits in her long white dress on rainy nights beside the Highway 70 underpass near Jamestown. New England has Peter Rugg, driving his carriage through the night, forever on his way to Boston but never quite arriving.

Folklore collector, Carl Carmer, writes about an ethereal girl in a lavender dress who haunts a stretch of road in the Ramapo River valley of New York State. The ancients supposed that after death men's souls wandered about the world disturbing the peace of its inhabitants. They called the good spirits *Lares familiares* and the evil ones *Lemurs*. These themes persist in both ancient and contemporary literature.

A human spirit, creature or event miraculously survives its moment in time to go on, perhaps, forever. The ghost hitchhiker on the mountain road near Walhalla may well be one of these spirits!

V.   Alice of the Hermitage

There are no other stories quite like this one, although, many are similar. There is the apparition of Caroline Neuffer of Poor Hope Plantation near Gaston, South Carolina; Charleston has its lady in white keeping her ghostly vigil on one of the balconies of a fine, old home. And at Edisto Island there is the bride of Brick House. Slain by a jealous suitor she died minutes before her wedding and it is said that in the eerie stillness of humid summer nights, a lady in shimmering white can be seen at the northwest window.

But Alice continues to have a reality about her that defies explanation. If it is true that there are roughly four categories of ghosts: crisis apparitions, purposive ghosts, wandering spirits, and ghosts of living people—Alice was one with a purpose. That purpose is the one that motivated her pathetic but determined efforts before she died, to obtain the ring her brother had forcibly taken from her.

She seems to have the freedom to visit her former home, The Hermitage, at will and has been seen near All Saints

Episcopal Church on the river near Pawleys Island and standing in the yard of the lovely old house where she died.

There are many cases in England where a ghost of some historical figure is said to haunt a manor or castle, but, in truth, no one has seen the ghost for years. The story may have arisen simply because a famous person lived or died there and such stories should be taken with some skepticism unless the ghost has been seen more recently.

In the case of Alice, who was certainly not a famous person, it makes the story more credible that accounts continue to be heard so many years after her death.

VI.   The Crazy Quilt

The story of the quilt is most unusual in this day and time, particularly since it is based on an occurrence in Kershaw, South Carolina, which was described in part by the Columbia newspaper, *The State*. Its origins might best be ascribed to man's most primitive past, a time of Märchens or fairy tales and the recovery of magical lost objects with special powers. Aladdin's lamp, the magic carpet and many other objects have possessed a power independent of their owners.

This phenomenon is also closely akin to poltergeist activities as evidenced by tugging and movement without human intervention, manifestations which are sometimes experienced in a most terrifying fashion.

Another theory that might be advanced is a psychological one: the two victims of the quilt's aggression share a quality that activates the quilt. The first person is the more normal in that she wishes to rid herself of the assaultive coverlet. The young man who receives it as a gift insists on wrestling with it to the point of destruction. Whatever the truth of the matter, one assumption is that the victim of a phenomenon of this sort may have a deep sense of guilt.

VII.   The Blue Lady of Hilton Head

How many violent deaths and how many tragedies have occurred to cause the appearance of such a multitude of spectral ladies?

There must be scores for the story of the Blue Lady walking near the old black metal lighthouse is similar to that of other celebrated ghosts. There are ghosts seen at the foot of a castle tower near the ruins of St. Andrews Cathedral at the seaport town of the same name in Scotland. One is a beautiful young lady dressed in a fourteenth-century gown and wearing long white gloves that reach to her elbows. Many have seen her walking up and down before the tower on wild and stormy nights.

When the Gray Lady of Camden, South Carolina, walked it was considered a harbinger of the death of some member of the family. In the English seaside town of Bognor there are still stories of the famous Dark Lady of Bognor who was always seen dressed in deepest mourning.

According to the Hilton Head story, the Blue Lady paces to and fro in the moonlight and is most often seen before approaching storms. Is this victim of misfortune still dreaming of her wretched death? Does she come back so that others may escape her fate? And, how can such appearances go on and on for centuries?

VIII.   The Convivial Spirit of Cool Springs

Warren Armstrong says that "Ghosts come and go as they please and take no humans into account in their hauntings." This is certainly the case in the cheerful spirit of Cool Springs Plantation.

Yes, there are "cheerful" ghosts. A delightful story of gay, hospitable ghosts was told in one Christmas issue of the British magazine, *The Countryman.* A bell ringer was greeted one cold, wintry night in the nave of the church by a ghost whose mausoleum stood nearby. In life named Sir Henry d'Epouvantail, Sir Henry's ghost spoke to the bell ringer saying, "Don't stand there with your teeth chattering, man. Come inside and have a drink." Whereupon a hitherto unseen door of the mausoleum opened and the man was hospitably ushered inside.

The spirit of a former owner of Cool Springs is said to return to his home on festive occasions and enjoy them as he did during the days he lived there. The present owners of the house pour a glass of wine and leave it as a cordial gesture for the apparition.

An interesting parallel occurs on the West Coast of Africa where the Ashanti tribesmen never drink without pouring a few drops of the wine on the ground for the denizens of the spirit world.

Ghosts are not always frightening. Often in both fact and fiction there are stories of the supernatural with nothing sinister about them. This would seem to be one of them, yet even these give us a sense of eeriness.

IX.   The Apparition at Anderson College

Along with haunted churches and convents there are many stories of haunted colleges and some military schools such as West Point and the Citadel where ghosts have reportedly been seen. To attempt to list them all would be an impossible undertaking. This story is intriguing because the ghost of the young girl appeared to be so real. The sight of her was probably even more unsettling as apparitions are seldom seen in the daytime.

The conversation with the ghost bears some similarity to one reported in England in 1949, the story of the haunting of the Bell House in Hertfordshire. The young woman in the music center at Anderson College comes back to search for her fiancé of years before. She is in that category of spirits who return to complete some important task or fulfill a strong desire.

It is interesting that several people who could have no possible emotional connection with the apparition speak with certainty about "something strange" in the building and say they have sensed "a presence."

X.   The Gray Man

The story of the Gray Man, like so many others, is based upon a tragedy yet he is more than just a benign ghost. He is purposive. But what altruism, what compassion would bring a spirit back year after year to warn of impending storms?

Stories of being warned by the Gray Man have come from many respected sources. If there was ever a contradiction to the belief that ghosts are by their very nature evil, the Gray Man should dispel this reputation. Stories have been told down through the generations to frighten children and, of course, there will always be those who take a certain delight in anything scarey.

The first chapter of Hebrews speaks of "ministering angels" and if we are to credit such a statement with any truth, some of us will surely encounter one. Could it be that those who meet the Gray Man have met a "ministering angel"?

XI.   Danger House

Objects in strange places, opening and closing doors, and all the small things the Browders noticed if taken together are certain indication that poltergeist activities existed in the Clark house. If confirmation were needed, the crashing sound of dishes followed by the discovery that all is in order is one of the more common poltergeist phenomena. In some

---

cases individuals have been suspected of provoking the manifestations. This is not to say that they were aware of it or were active instigators but rather that their personality or emotions released an uncontrolled and chaotic form of energy. Often, when the individual left, the events ceased.

At the Borley Rectory in England, events took place not only during the visit of the sometimes maligned and sometimes commended Harry Price, but also after he left. The wife of the Reverend G. E. Smith was compelled to admit that odd things happened. Mrs. Smith heard the rectory gates open and saw the headlamps of some vehicle in the darkness outside, but there was no vehicle. Her husband found doors and windows mysteriously opened. Sir Ernest Bennett carefully documented occurrences of this nature in *Apparitions and Haunted Houses* (1939).

Concerning the footsteps and the lady rocking on the porch, evidence indicates their behavior to be somnambulistic or automatic. The pattern of the footsteps was probably predetermined long before the Browders moved into the house in this case.

The incidents of almost spontaneous combustion raise the question of hostile acts. The extremely superstitious could blame some evil force. On the other hand, faulty wiring or Browder's own generation of electrical wavelengths might have ignited the fires. It is certainly something of a coincidence that both fires occurred in his immediate proximity.

XII.   The Specter of the Slaughter Yards

Ghosts most often appear because of some event, sad or joyous, that burns itself into the human consciousness. It does not have to be tragic but in this instance it was and the story traces the threads of evil to their horrifying conclusion.

This account was gleaned from newspaper files or related to the writer by people deeply involved from start to finish.

One was Tessie Earle; another took part in that early morning drama on February 17, 1947. Some names have been changed to prevent embarrassment.

Someone may ask, why does the author write this story? Because the chain of events in this story created a ghost. The return of the ghost of Willie Earle fits a common pattern. In almost every culture when a person dies a violent death it is thought that the spirit of the victim returns to haunt the place of the tragedy. And such is the case with the story of the return of a man named Willie Earle.

XIII. The Hound of Goshen

There have been stories of fierce, supernatural dogs as far back as the memory of man. In the time of the ancient Greeks, the Hound of Hell, Cerberus, was believed to lie chained at the gates of Hades where he devoured both intruders from the outside world and anyone trying to escape from the underworld.

The murderess, Hecuba, wife of the king of Troy, changed into a dog when pursued by an angry mob. Later we read of the fearsome Black Shuck of East Anglia, the Padfoot of Yorkshire and the pooka, a huge, black, furry dog, one of the spirits of Ireland and Wales that attaches itself to someone and follows wherever they go but is unseen by anyone else.

Then, there was the famous gray dog drowned at sea that Sir Walter Scott immortalized. Its ghost was a monstrous creature with eyes like glowing coals and it roamed the cliffs of Scarba in the Hebrides.

American blacks have their own stories and in South Carolina the Gullahs talk of the plat-eye. Never a dog at all in real life, it was always the ghost of some unfortunate who had been carelessly buried. The ghost was said to appear on lonely roads at night in the shape of an animal called a plat-eye, often a dog with fiery eyes.

Whether grounded in Biblical verses from the eleventh chapter of Exodus or not, the superstition has long prevailed that a howling dog is an omen of death. Thus we know there have been many ancestors of the spectral Hound of Goshen. But we do not know why he is seen only by certain people or when he will appear. We can only wonder whether this very night, near the ruins of the fire-ravaged Douglass house, an immense white hound may be loping from the Stygian darkness to follow someone down the old Buncombe Road.

XIV.   There Goes Martin Baynard's Carriage

The story of sightings of Martin Baynard's carriage has a striking counterpart in England. One of the most famous phantom coaches is connected with Wool Bridge Manor made familiar by Thomas Hardy's *Tess of the D'Urbervilles*. The coach, as recent as the eighteenth century in design, would begin its reckless ride at dusk from Wool Bridge Manor to Bere Regis drawn by four horses. Supposedly, it is the result of an earlier murder and for those unfortunate enough to see it, the phantom coach is an omen of death or disaster.

New England has a legend of a horse-drawn carriage driven by a man named Peter Rugg. Travelers would meet him on stormy, rainy nights riding as fast as a thundercloud. Wet and weary, the tragic man drives on forever, never able to reach his home and frightening those he meets.

A similar story is often heard today. In Pennsylvania Dutch country a car starts up a hill and as it reaches the crest, the horrified driver sees a covered wagon in the moonlight on the down side of the hill just ahead of him—a wagon he is convinced he will crash into and demolish! It is impossible to stop and he cannot believe it when he drives right through the wagon. A ghost or an illusion from the past?

Appearances such as this have been reported near the scene of fatal accidents. In 1933 stories of a "ghost bus" began to spread in North Kensington, London, and fortunate for the sanity of those who had seen it, there were other witnesses. The phantom bus was invariably seen hurtling by in the early morning hours. It took on a frightening aspect when it was encountered at the dangerous crossing of St. Mark's Road and Cambridge Gardens where there had been numerous fatal accidents.

Drivers would swerve violently to avoid it, one car crashing into the wall of a house. Dozens of Kensington residents talked about being awakened by the roar of a bus late at night after all service had stopped. When they rushed to their window they would see a brilliantly lighted but completely empty bus approaching.

These accounts are all of the same genre as the story of Martin Baynard's carriage. Sometimes the ghosts seen at places like this linger on for years.

XV.   The Singing Portrait

This story is more of a poltergeist story than the conventional ghost story. What causes poltergeist activity? Dr. Nandor Fodor, psychoanalyst and member of the New York Academy of Science as well as the holder of other positions of prestige, is an expert on this phenomenon.

Fodor says we believe that the poltergeist is a bundle of projected repression or frustration. He goes on to say that tremendous energy is released but we do not know the nature of this energy. Is it musuclar, nervous, electric or electronic? How does it work?

He theorizes that the human body is capable of releasing energy in a manner similar to atomic bombardments. The atom has no power to give direction to this energy but a human being has. Under strong emotion this discharge takes place. It is a product of the psyche of the projector rather than the conscious mind.

Ordinarily this is caused unconsciously by someone in the proximity of the poltergeist activity, but he does mention an interesting alternative. This is the haunting by the living from a distance. He quotes the case of a George Walton who cheated a widow out of her land. Bent locks and bars occurred and there were tappings on his windows. There is also a strong resemblance to the famous Bell Witch story of Tennessee.

Walton's house, however, had belonged to the widow and strong emotions may still have been present there.

We can speculate that the emotional energy was released unconsciously by Joseph Newton or that in some mysterious way, "Miss Anna" was able to project sufficient energy to make the portrait of herself pulsate with life.

XVI.   The Spirit with the Tradd Street Address

This is a story about a very unostentatious, quiet, introverted sort of ghost. A ghost that prefers not to bother anyone, but would rather slip down the stairs unaccompanied by the rattle of chains, pause for a moment to see if she is observed, and then go out the front door.

When the ghost's footsteps can be heard from downstairs, it no doubt embarrasses her that she may have drawn some attention. If she is not as violent or colorful as some and reappears only because she once lived in, perhaps, loved this house, we must forgive and welcome a pause in the pace of violence and tragedy.

The owner of the home has coped with her uninvited guest in a gracious manner. This is a true story contributed by a lady who is living in Charleston. I believe it. It is also my belief that there are many old Charleston homes with their ghostly presences if one is sensitive enough to perceive them.

XVII.   The Ghost of Daufuskie Island

Although, the ghost of the old man with the white beard seemed to enjoy a special friendship with Nick, the rest of the Beatty family saw him too. He was seen in the kitchen and on another occasion walking through the yard. If this were not the case, it would be tempting to dismiss this story by placing it in the "imaginary playmate" category, an experience common to many of us at some time in our childhood.

Unseen hands that knock are more often heard of than visible chairs that rock, as did the one in the Beatty living room. This is similar to a current British story of an empty cradle that persists in rocking in an ancient house in Yorkshire, England.

Apparitions are seldom frightening and often give warnings or speak. The apparition of Arthur Burns shares the characteristic of purposiveness in that he had decided before he died that he would never leave this house.

The spirit of Rupert Brooke, one of England's poet heroes, is said to return often to the home he loved. The house is called the Old Vicarage and he wrote a poem about it. Here is no frightening ghost but rather a gentle man who died for his country in World War I. This bears a resemblance to the return of Arthur Burns.

On the other hand, did the spirit of Arthur find a sympathetic soul in young Nick out there in the old cemetery and decide to go home with him? Of course, that speculation could be based upon a belief that the spirits of the deceased may sometimes be present in the cemetery where they have been buried.

XVIII.   The Phantom Horseman of Columbia

The Columbia phenomenon bears striking similarities to numerous instances of the sightings of "Angel Horses." In early Jewish history there are at least three occasions of a heavenly horse and rider coming to the assistance of the hard-pressed Jews. The apocryphal second book of Maccabee contains three fascinating accounts of angel horses being seen on earth.

These appearances were often associated with wars. During the conflict between the Spaniards and Moors, the Christians had besieged the stronghold of Coimbra unsuccessfully for seven months when St. James appeared to a pilgrim and promised to give his aid. The following day the soldiers saw an unknown warrior among them on a snow-white steed who led the charge wherever the battle was fiercest. Before evening they had conquered the citadel of the Moors.

At Gettysburg the soldiers of the 20th Maine were on Little Round Top almost out of ammunition and about to lose a crucial position. The men were led by a figure on a white charger who they were convinced was General Washington. They followed him to victory.

When the British fought the Germans at Mons against fearful odds, an apparition was seen by both English and Germans alike. In terror the Germans abandoned their position and fled. The British were convinced it was St. George, the patron saint of England. In other instances men wrote of seeing "Clouds of Celestial Horsemen" hovering over British lines.

General Skobeleff, a Russian national hero, appeared to soldiers on a snowy charger to warn them of coming peril. In similar circumstances the French sometimes saw Joan of Arc mounted on a magnificent white horse. These stories were taken very seriously and ghost horsemen were often deemed prophetic. The color white meant brightness and symbolized the holy and spiritual nature. In Revelations 19: 11–14, Christ appears on a white horse, the emblem of conquest, with the armies of heaven following upon white horses.

In Ireland, Killarney was once supposedly haunted by the ghosts of the hero O'Donoghue and his favorite horse, and for many years after his death his spirit is said to have been seen on his ghostly steed. It may well be that before World War I, the Phantom Horseman seen riding in the sky over Columbia was, indeed, the spirit of General Wade Hampton.

Bibliography

Armstrong, Warren. *The Authenitic Shudder*. John Day Co., New York, 1967.

Bord, Janet. *Ghosts*. David & Charles, Inc., North Pomfret, Vt., 1974.

Brown, Frank C. *The Frank C. Brown Collection of North Carolina Folklore*. 7 vols. Duke University Press, Durham, 1952.

Cavendish, Richard. *Encyclopedia of the Unexplained*. McGraw-Hill Book Co., New York, 1974.

Clark, Joseph D. *Beastly Folklore*. Scarecrow Press, Inc., Metuchen, N.J., 1964.

Editors of Life. *The Life Treasury of American Folklore*. Time, Inc., New York, 1961.

Fodor, Nandor. *Between Two Worlds*. Parker Publishing Co., West Nyack, N.Y. 1964.

————. *On the Trail of the Poltergeist*. Citadel Press, New York, 1958.

Georgia Writers Project. *Drums and Shadows*. Reprint Company, Spartanburg, S.C., 1974.

Green, Patricia. *Lore of the Dog*. Houghton Mifflin Co., Boston, 1967.

Harter, Walter. *The Phantom Hand and Other American Hauntings*. Prentice-Hall, Inc., Englewood Cliffs, N.J., 1976.

Howery, M. Oldenfield. *The House of Magic and Myth*. Castle Books, New York, 1968.

Jackson, Bruce. *The Negro and His Folklore*. University of Texas Press, Austin, 1967.

Leach, Maria. *God Had a Dog*. Rutgers University Press, New Brunswick, N.J., 1961.

Ludlam, Harry. *The Restless Ghosts of Lodge Place*. Taplinger, New York, 1968.

Roberts, Nancy. *An Illustrated Guide to Ghosts*. McNally & Loftin, Charlotte, N.C., 1959, 1967.

————. *Ghosts of the Southern Mountains and Appalachia*. University of South Carolina Press, Columbia, S.C., 1989.

————. *Ghosts of the Carolinas*. University of South Carolina Press, Columbia, S.C., 1988.

————. *This Haunted Southland*. University of South Carolina Press, Columbia, S.C., 1988.

————. *Southern Ghosts*. Doubleday & Company, New York, 1979.

Rugoff, Milton. *A Harvest of World Folk Tales*, Viking Press, New York, 1949.